The Sound of Rattles and Clappers

» » The Sound of
Rattles and Clappers

A Collection of New California Indian Writing

Edited by Greg Sarris

The University of Arizona Press / Tucson

The University of Arizona Press
Copyright © 1994
The Arizona Board of Regents
All rights reserved

♾ This book is printed on acid-free, archival-quality paper.
Manufactured in the United States of America

99 98 97 96 95   6 5 4 3 2

Library of Congress Cataloging-in-Publication Data

The Sound of rattles and clappers : a collection of new California
Indian writing / edited by Greg Sarris.
    p.   cm. — (Sun tracks ; v. 26)
ISBN 0-8165-1280-9 (cl : acid-free paper). — ISBN 0-8165-1434-8
(pb : acid-free paper)
1. Indians of North America—California—Literary collections.
2. American literature—Indian authors.   3. American literature—
20th century.   4. American literature—California.   I. Sarris, Greg.
II. Series.
PS508.I5S63   1994   93-43864
810.8'08970794—dc20   CIP

British Cataloguing-in-Publication Data
A catalogue record for this book is available from the British Library.

Contents

Frank LaPena/Tauhindauli

James Luna

Stephen Meadows

Introduction
The Sound of Rattles and Clappers

One day in early spring I drove with Mabel McKay to the hills above Clear Lake in northern California. We parked on an old road well above the lake where there was a view of the water and steep, oak-dotted hills beyond. I was surprised when Mabel got out of the car. The weather was damp and cold and Mabel was getting on in years, over eighty. Grabbing my notebook and pen, I hurried out of the car and joined her in the drizzling rain. All afternoon I had been attempting to write down what she was telling me, stories that I had heard from her most of my life. People wanted to know about this renowned Cache Creek Pomo medicine woman and basket weaver, so I figured that if I was going to write and publish her stories, I better get them straight.

But Mabel wasn't saying anything just then.

I waited. Nothing. The heavy drizzle soaked my notebook, swelled the time and date on the page. Dew collected in Mabel's hair and covered her glasses. I wondered how she could see.

Then I found out.

She was facing east, toward Long Valley. I assumed that when she started talking it would be about the village place there and what her grandmother had told her. But it wasn't about that at all. She talked about Sulfur Bank, directly below us, near the water, about how her grandmother had danced with the people of that place after white settlers forced the Long Valley Cache Creek Pomo off their land. Mabel had gone to Sulfur Bank with her grandmother and participated in the old-time Bole Maru and Big Head ceremonies. She danced in the Roundhouse, holding on to her grandmother's skirt. Her grandmother was often sad, but when the old woman came to Sulfur Bank she was a different person, happy and light. Mabel could see the change in her grandmother's face as the horses pulled their wagon out of the eastern hills and into the village. There was a place on the road, a bend where you could hear the sounds of people singing before you could see the village. "And the clappers," Mabel said, taking the glasses from her face. "Them clappers," she repeated, her eyes bright, concentrated. "Them clappers sounding loud, echoing in these hills, echoing everywhere so the people would know."

Today, more than eighty years since that time when Mabel was a small girl with her grandmother, California Indian peoples are still dancing, singing, telling stories. You can hear the sharp clacking of split elderberry clappers in the central regions of the state, and in the south the steady rhythm of gourd-rattles. Skirts with abundant and beautiful shells shake and sound on the women of the northwest. All of us California Indians come from a place, a tribal location. Even if we never lived on or near that place, most of us have heard the stories. These places and the stories associated with them anchor us no matter how far we travel. That spot on the narrow old road above Clear Lake is one such place for me.

I wanted to gather the work of these writers in a single collection for two reasons: first, because so much of the writing speaks to me of my own history and experience; and second, because I wanted other American Indians and non-Indians to see and hear the voices of California Indians. By California Indians I mean here American Indians of California Indian ancestry. I know this definition is arbitrary and limiting. Certainly there are American Indians in California who may be third- or fourth-generation "Californian" and consider California their home. And I am aware that a couple of the writers in this collection are not presently living in the state. Because of the limited amount of space in this one book, I had to make decisions, and I wanted to start with the place, the original people of the place, and find out what we have to say about it.

The writers in this volume document history, illuminating aspects of our respective native cultures and charting our travels in time and space. Vine Deloria, Jr., wrote that modern Indian poetry can "tell you more about the Indian's travels in historical experience than all the books written and lectures given." So it is with the poetry and prose of California Indian writers. So much of what we have witnessed and continue to live with is painful, horrendous. In her poem "History Lesson," Janice Gould chronicles the brutal history of her Maidu people, taking the reader from the tribe's decimation by diseases brought by the European invaders to the present, where a lone Maidu girl attempts to tell her history in a classroom of uncaring students. Frank LaPena, in "Red Pond," writes of the Bloody Island Massacre of Pomo in Lake County:

Comes the morning
when the blood of dead
lay silent
floating in the
red red water

And in "Splashes of Red, Autumn 1867," Darryl Babe Wilson says:

The odor of scorched gunpowder
    filled the air
In the morning
    it lay in soft, blue clouds
        over the earth of my people

The isolation and alienation of a contemporary California Indian is perhaps never more painfully realized than in James Luna's "The Artifact Piece," in which an Indian's (Luna's) body is displayed in a museum with an adjoining text describing events "during days of [his] excessive drinking."

The painful experiences of our history affords us a sharp eye as critics of histories and situations beyond the confines of our own places and tribes. In "We Live!" Wendy Rose writes of the situation of so many American Indians in this country. We live, she says,

circling down
to textbook pages
dyed with our blood,
red and wet

> from the slip
> of white tongues;
> in museums
> our bones exposed
> to weep and howl
> to clatter helplessly

Stephen Meadows, in his poem "At the Crossing," describes logging practices common in all too many places: "A chainsaw dismembers the silence / of a white afternoon."

Despite the pain, and amidst what Ken Lincoln has called "the acute aftermath of shock, the aching silences of delayed stress," these writers speak of endurance, of traditions and family that persist against all odds. In "Round Valley Songs" William Oandasan hears and dreams the old Yuki songs:

> from fresh currents of night air
> above manzanitas near the cemetery
> the words of ancient lips
> turn in our blood again
>
> long ago black bears
> sang around our lodge fires
> tonight they dance
> alive through our dreams

In "Grandmothers Land" William celebrates the "five generations" of his Grandmother Jessie: "after spreading to the four directions / the seeds of Jessie have returned." Likewise, Georgiana Sanchez, in "A Light to Do Shellwork By," lauds the life of her father even as she tells of his dying:

> The ocean sang in my father's hands
> abalone pendants shimmered rainbows
> from the ears of pretty girls
>
> and shellwork dotted driftwood carvings
> > cowrie shells, cone shells, volute shells
> > red, black, white, blue, brown, green shells
> the life they once held
> sacred

old stories etched on
the lifeline of my father's palm

In "Chumash Man" Georgiana writes of her father's insistence that he is Chumash despite the U.S. government's claim that the tribe has been "terminated." Kathleen Smith fondly remembers her family as she relates favorite family recipes, which keep alive not only certain Pomo and Coast Miwok traditions associated with the preparation of foods but also an entire family and tribal history.

Indeed, what characterizes so much of the work by these writers is a profound love of place and people. It is a love that covers all that is human, from love for one's family and friends to romantic love for one's lover. Perhaps the latter is no better told than in Janice Gould's "To Speak Your Name":

To hold you deeper
than you have been held,
find the cry in your throat,
loosen what is lodged
in the marrow of bone and flesh,
to touch you everywhere I am
open is what I love. You
sing for me now
in your soft southern voice.

From this place called California, then, you have the voices of many California Indians. They are singing, telling stories, their voices echoing on the pages so you will know. Listen. This place, these rolling, oak-dotted hills, redwood forests, deserts and ocean shores are sounding.

In closing this introduction I want to extend my personal gratitude to Larry Evers and Ofelia Zepeda, co-editors of the University of Arizona Press's Sun Tracks series, for publishing this anthology. And I want to thank my fellow California Indian people, not only those who write, particularly the wonderful writers who have contributed to this volume, but those people who tell us stories, give us so much to write about. I live in Los Angeles now, far from my Coast Miwok and Kashaya Pomo family in Sonoma County. A few months ago I attended a gathering of Southern California Cahuilla people who sang old Cahuilla bird songs. They marked the beat with gourd-rattles. I listened, and later that night I thought of home and heard our songs and clappers. Like these writers, the Cahuilla people remind me of my place, where I come from.

GREG SARRIS

The Sound of Rattles and Clappers

» » Janice Gould

Janice Gould's tribal affiliation is koyangk'auwi (Konkow), but she is listed on the tribal roll as Maidu. At the University of California at Berkeley she studied American Indian languages while majoring in linguistics. After earning a master's degree in English at Berkeley, she entered the doctoral program in American Studies at the University of New Mexico and later transferred to the English program to work more intensively in American Indian literature. Her first volume of poetry is *Beneath My Heart*.

» Coyotismo

My mother lay on her side to birth me.
This was millennia ago
when the earth was still fresh
with the energy of being.

I was her first.
If any came before me,
they were lies and unwanted.

We were poor, I was hungry.
You can't imagine the places I've begged:
beaches, city streets, conference tables.
I will eat garbage,
but not from anyone's hand.

We were poor, I was cold.
Mama made me a coat but no trousers.
People laughed at me.
I was always angry.

They joked about my sex,
said nasty things about my genitalia.
I became vengeful.

Once I heard the moon whisper behind my back.
I scooped hot coals
and threw them in her fat face.
Sure, it burned my hands—
but she is marked with permanent surprise.

Another time the night began a rumor
that I'd hump anything that moved.
What did she know? When she opened her mouth to laugh,
I pulled her tongue real hard.
She vomited a trail of stars no one can clean up.

I know more than I can say!
No poetry exists which wasn't first on my lips.
I was a live seed planted by a woman
in another woman's womb.
All things insatiable belong to me.

» Children Who Never Departed

In Alaska, in the long summer twilight,
it may be when the wind's in the aspen,
the quaking leaves awaken

two Indian children
buried above the Salcha River.

They fly straight up from the grave,
and their souls wrap around each other
like a whirlwind.
Their grief falls
on the white stars of dogwood,
on spruce and willow
that bank the calm river.

Sometimes you may see them
when, picking high-bush cranberries,
you sweat to the crest of a bluff.
They stand quietly at the edge of the glade,
or lie clasping one another
amid moss and matted roots
in damp exploded earth.

» Doves

Our lives go on viscerally, austere, beneath our memories. You are the girl with bruised knees, her summer dress spattered with blood, grief, shame, and a man's sperm, something torn as he pushes you down on the heap of clean laundry you carried home that evening, walking barefoot on the street. I am the child who examines the body of a mourning dove in its shoebox, feathers colored ivory and blue beneath pale brown. Kneeling in the woods where moss and tall grasses grow, we know how to pray, how to have a funeral. I don't want to go there alone, or to the shed where, in the dark, bicycles are stored, and old rope.

» History Lesson

A terrible pestilence, an intermittent fever, was reported as having almost depopulated the whole valley of Sacramento and San Joaquin. . . . The country was strewn with the remains of the dead wherever a village had stood, and from the headwaters of the Sacramento to King's River only five Indians were seen.

HUBERT HOWE BANCROFT

1832

All this fall we have watched our families sicken
with astonishing rapidity. In a fever they chill to the bone,
then break into a profuse sweat. The shuddering heat and cold
alternates till they are too weak to rise from where they lay
and simply die. In our village no adults are left,
just one woman so heartbroken she can do nothing
but wail and smear her shorn head with pitch.
The children not stricken with fever neither sleep nor eat,
they are frightened and grieving, for the dead
clamor about us, even in this silence,
and poison the air with their stench.
There are too many to bury. We must wander away.
We cannot stay here.

Wandering, I thought I would feel no more.
Then I came to a place that filled me with disgust and shame
though at first only confusion and fear.
The skinned carcasses of hundreds of elk
lay swelling in the rain
at the foot of the Buttes.
Two white men lived there in a canvas tent.
Up they panted when they saw me
and pointed their guns at my chest.
If I escaped it is only with a prayer,
for it seems they kill everything that goes about on legs,
and upon doing this, cut away and take the skin
and leave the meat to rot for black-winged birds of prey.

1849

General Bidwell has hired us to work at his gold diggings
on the Feather River. If we work well, we'll be paid
two red handkerchiefs a day.
Otherwise we'll be paid but one.

1851

Several headmen among us Maidu have signed a treaty
with the white government.

We are to stay on the land between Chico and Oroville,
clear up to Nimshew, and we are not to stray.

For this the men will receive a pair of jeans,
a red flannel shirt, and a plow.
Women will get a linsey gown,
a few yards of calico, scissors and thread.

1852

At first we could not understand how the whites could settle on the land granted us by the Treaty. They came in droves. Then we learned the U.S. Senate had secretly rejected all treaties with Maidu and other Indian tribes, and we were to be removed to Nome Lackie reservation, several miles away.

1863

They told us, *Because of conflict between Indians and whites, you will be moved for your own safety to Round Valley Reservation. It is in Mendocino County, some three days march away.*

The removal has taken two weeks,
and of the 461 Indians who began this miserable trek,
only 277 have come to Round Valley.
Many died as follows: Men were shot who tried to escape.
The sick, or old, or women with children
were speared if they could not keep up,
bayonets being used to conserve ammunition.
Babies were also killed, taken by the feet
and swung against trees or rocks to crack their skulls.

1984

There are some things I don't want to talk about.
That chapter, for example, on California Indians which read:
California Indians were a naturally shiftless and lazy people. The Mission padres had no trouble bringing them into the Mission for these Indians were more submissive than the Plains warriors.
California Indians were easily conquered.

When mama was brought to the city,
she heard a neighbor remark,
"Why did they ever adopt an Indian? Don't they know
Indians are too dumb to learn anything?"
Mama said, "I'll show her!" and went off to Julliard and Columbia.
But when she came back to marry my dad,
her future mother-in-law turned to him and said,
"Why, she speaks English as well as we do!"

Mama used to say, "Why can't you kids learn anything?
What's wrong with you? Are you too dumb?
Perhaps you're just lazy and stupid.
Why don't you do as well as your friends?
Why do you give up? Why do you want to fail?
Why don't you make the effort?"
But how could we answer?

Sometimes I wake up in the night, clenching my fists, crying.
This morning it was because when I had to report about
Christopher Columbus, the whole class turned away, bored,
and began to talk amongst themselves.
"Christopher Columbus," I began, "had two motives
behind his voyage. He was intrigued by the discovery
of hitherto unknown languages,
and by the discovery of skull shapes and sizes
unlike the European."
Here I held up a small discolored skull, then continued,
"Christopher Columbus meant to sail around the world
until he found a language
with a shape which matched its sounds."
I held up an alphabet in beautiful calligraphy.

I knew the class did not care
and I raged into a frenzy, beating desktops,
throwing chairs aside.
The professor got up to leave the room,
her eyes sad and frightened.
I glared at her.

"You can finish your talk," she said,
"when you pull yourself together."

I stood in a corner of the room
and cried in humiliation and grief.

» We Exist

For Beth Brant

Indians must be the loneliest people on Earth—
lonely from our histories,
our losses,
even those things we cannot name
which are inside us.
Our writers try to counteract the history
that says we are dead, a conquered People.
But our words are like a shout in a blizzard.

In snow one December,
those at Wounded Knee lay dying,
dead, their bodies frozen open.
Soldiers dug a ditch
for the bodies.
Then prairie soil crumbled over the People,
and their hearts fed on roots and stones.
Their mouths filled with dust.
At sunrise the daughter lies on the bed,
legs drawn up, fist in her mouth.
I am poisoned, she thinks, beneath my heart.
This is what it means to be Indian.
My mother is not here.
They mined her for her grief,
following each vein, invading
every space, removing, they said,
the last vestige of pain.

At dawn, this time of prayer, the daughter
in a voice mined from a sickness of soul,

tries to name the words
which say we exist.

» **Alphabet**

A is a mountain
whose steep ascent
leads to a pinnacle
from which you can view
the extent of these shapes.
B is for flesh,
the letter of home.
C is the first coil of a basket,
and a severed ear.
D is the belly of the moon
or a bear.
E represents three paths
from the main road.
One path leads to an inner place.
F hobbles on one foot,
while G rolls upon the dusty earth.
H shows the banks of a canal
crossed by a narrow bridge
in winter.
I is solitary.
J is a jack to the king's K
who is really a knave.
L is the right angle of pain.
M is a fish
swimming toward heaven,
while N plunges toward darkness.
O opens and illumines the night.
P is proud and pedantic
Q is a monkey's cage,
his tail the only thing free.
R is the sailor's device,

having to do with sextants
and stars.
S leads to the Milky Way,
or earthbound becomes the vine
that circles a tree.
T stands for the forest
where the most mysterious letters
live in huts and caves.
U sends you back
the way you came.
V is the meteor's descent,
W the neighbor's fence,
while X marks a crossroad
where you decide: Christian
or Pagan?
Y represents choice.
Z is the zigzag of the path back home,
or away.

» When Winter Hits Lake Erie

When winter hits Lake Erie and sleets the town,
the small dead lie frozen by the side of the road.
Nothing remains but torn wings, teeth,
bits of fur, and cracked bones.

When winter hits Lake Erie, you lie curled
in the ice cave which blankets your bed.
I sleep a thousand miles away in a winter all my own,

and wake to the half-human cries of coyote.
It is an effort of will to cup my hands on the window,
to peer into the dark where tracks cross the snow.

» To Speak Your Name

To speak your name
between your warm thighs

above the curve of your belly
in the cave of your mouth
close to your closing eyes,
this is what I want.
My kisses scatter
like migrating birds
over your breasts.

To hold you deeper
than you have been held,
find the cry in your throat,
loosen what is lodged
in the marrow of bone and flesh,
to touch you everywhere I am
open is what I love. You
sing for me now
in your soft southern voice.

» Blackbirds

At dusk we start home
through the wet fields.

Overhead, blackbirds flock
and flock, coming together

like the sides of a squeeze-box,
scattering apart, a rush

of stars navigating
their own universe.

The birds whisper in the damp air,
their wings breathe.

When you take my hand
I feel the pulse of their flight

in my throat, my chest.
I feel their pull

flutter through you.

» Three Stories from My Mother

Prayer Path
We stand beneath the buckeye tree,
and the big pods rattle in the wind.
Blind grandma listens and sometimes sings
in a voice already like a ghost's.
Her hand rests on my shoulder;
I am her eyes.
I shift my weight and strain to hear
the voices she attends.

Grandma has staked the other world to our own.
The day she leaves, no longer blind,
she will follow a trail of feathers,
tassels hung to elderberry,
knots of long, bent grass.
She will walk quickly
like a young thing
down the dim trail.

Cure Night
Mama became very sick
when something puffed in her side
like a boil.
Her limbs were soft-boned,
her eyes pockets of pain.
Finally she had no voice
to call us from play,
so she lay down
and began to wait for death.
Papa rode out of the canyon
and brought the medicine man from Humbug Valley.
The old man chanted that night,
shaking the deerskin rattle.
He blew smoke across mama
and sucked at her sore side,

trying to draw between his teeth
what remained swollen in her.

Late in the night he stopped singing,
and in the silence
we heard the crackle of fire,
the hiss as lamps burned low.

Wind dragged itself down the creek
and seeped into the rafters of our house.
Words came in a strange high language.

The old man sighed and turned to my father,
saying no Indian medicine could change
the day of her last breath.

She Comes Home

Dad took mama up to Quincy.
White doctors removed the tumor.
Maybe because she was a half-breed
they were careless how they sewed her up.
They sent her home on the train.

Her life slipped away
as the Southern Pacific snaked down the canyon.
Its brakes groaned on the long grades,
and a hemorrhage appeared on the folds
of mama's cotton dress.
There was heat glare
on mica and serpentine.

Perhaps she watched the river,
the way it bucks and eddies
and swirls in the deep pools.
Perhaps she took in the deep blue of the sky,
noticed wind catching in the aspen,
saw patches of snow saddling the razor-backed ridges.
It was thirty miles of pain
to where we kids were waiting.

At Belden station
the men strapped her to a chair
and carried her into town.
Already she was moaning
in a voice so changed and low
it belonged to no woman.

In that sound she drifted,
unaware it was death who sang.

» Questions of Healing

In Dorothy Hill's The Fauna and Flora of the Mountain Maidu,
I turn a page and discover
the healing properties of cedar,
elderberry and spruce,
of deer hooves, eagles' bones, and sage.

In times past,
all things helped the People survive.
For each thing that harmed—
rattler, poison oak, grizzly bear, lightning—
another thing existed to cure, arrest poison,
reverse madness, disease, or death.

To imagine that the world could exist
so finely balanced!
Each day to strike fire from a stone
and watch clouds gather at the canyon's edge.
To see smoke rise from the volcano
and believe in the rightness
and clear gifts of the earth.
To calmly face our own aging—
how strange and inaccessible.

When I watched my mother die
with no recourse to laurel,
sweet birch or pine, no baskets
to burn on the pyre in October (ourselves

the sticks of charcoal, shaved heads,
black face, purified by smoke),
I found only half-questions:
What in our world? How close to death?
What can change? What have I lost?

» Last Journey

Mama left for the mountains
on the first of September.
She traveled west to east,
an old journey through manzanita,
sage and rabbit brush.

In canyons, oak leaves shimmered
in dry heat,
cones dropped from sugar pines
in a scatter of small brown wings.
Mama followed a streambed
of flat white stones.

When you passed the Buttes, mama,
did you pray for your daughters,
whose way to the meadows above
might be difficult?

Up there, beyond black mesas
and eroded cliffs,
is the red earth country
of our home.

» Beneath My Heart

I felt the soul move within my body
and placed my hands over my heart,

but my soul drifted
effortlessly out of my grasp.

It hovered above me like a shadow
caught in a leafless tree.

Below my breast I searched,
trying to find the heart's beat.

Grace drags the soul,
deadened like a numb foot,

out of its earthlike sleep,

while light, heavy as flame,
breaks through the trees.

Beneath my heart a torrent of blood
carries all that I love.

When mama dies I will turn
like a star learning to shine,

the world will release me
into its vastness.

When death comes rapping with its soft claw,
I will stand in the doorway,
then leave.

» » Frank LaPena/Tauhindauli

Frank LaPena is a professor of Art and Ethnic Studies, and Director of
Native American Studies at California State University, Sacramento. He is
an artist and writer and is involved in traditional ceremony and dance.
LaPena has written some of his work under his Wintu name, Tauhindauli.
He has been an artist for more than thirty years.

» There was a time when the stars fell like rain. It was in the year of 1833.
The Wintu tribe speak of this time in reference to our last battle with the
Shasta tribe from the north; and they talk of the consequences of that star
fall.

> Around the time
> of the "falling stars"
> the Shasta were defeated
> for the last time
> by the Wintu
>
> On the ridge at
> the western rim

Widemcanus killed
the Shasta war leader
with the yellow throat

"Look," the storyteller said
"it went from here . . ."
his fingers traced
the jawline, under
the chin and down
the throat

Many Shasta were killed
and later death
turned and came
to the Wintu

The malaria epidemic
of 1833 killed 75 percent
of the people and
those left were overwhelmed
by the numbers of the dead.
They could only sorrow
in the grief

The smell of death filled the air
forcing survivors to burn
or leave the bodies unburied.
A village became known
as "stench flesh"
because it was impossible
to bury the rotting bodies

It was a hard
and difficult time
We remember it as the time
of falling stars

» I Am Stone of Many Colors

I am stone of many colors
some colors heal
while others
speak of madness

My surface is mirror
to the universe
and just causes
turned to sand
but still existing
feeling rain, and sun
and wind

We must always remember
we are sacred
our messages
hidden by lost
references and symbols

Like man
we are
eternal in one sense
vulnerable in the next

» Wrapped Hair Bundles

The birds turned
stopping
the flow of things
reminding me of
dream times
hair cutting times
when grief wraps
small bundles
of hair

It's all right
to stop and shake
his hand
"How are things, Peeny?"

Trying to show how
things really are
his father cuts
his hair
in a shawl of white
and he in turn
has his hair cut

For bundles
to show
how death takes
gifts of hair
and makes
itself a shawl

» The Year of Winter

The image of earth
in winter
is what is remembered
with grey sage figures
showing here and there

Winter gave them ice
river roads
and people moved them
on the bones of Winter
ribbon highways

The rivers were crossed
and recrossed
by wading people
going for riverbanks
that vanished in the spring thaw

Silent as guide
column stones
the people sat
like stacked stones
upright in the
spring melt

An elder hugged the skull
of his ancestors and wept
openly and unashamed

The sweet smell of flesh
was coming alive
with the melting snow

The earth was covered
with the bones of winter
for as far as the eye could see

» Waiting for a Second Time

my friend cannot speak anymore
but he knows everything we say
and everything we're thinking
he had a stroke and fell
and was found wandering around
like a bloodied punch-drunk fighter
trying to make things right again

I saw him on the second day
with tubes of saline juice
feeding him moisture
which he never wanted or cared for
his body protested
being immobilized in his metal bed
though the stroke guaranteed
a certain immobility
he was tied down to
"insure his safety"

I looked into his eyes
and recalled the times
we talked about getting old
and how "a damned shame
it was to fall down, break arms

and legs and lose the ability
to keep a good hard on"
"it's hell on the woman, it's
hell on the man," old age even
stopped one from remembering
what herb to take
for such disorders

I hoped he remembered those
stories for they had that humorous
side only the afflicted can appreciate
the nurse complained he never
ate for them but did for us
as she gave him his potassium
in tomato juice

the heart medicine uses up the
body's supply of potassium
and orange juice and tomato juice
are used to ease its bitterness
if getting old is to lose one's
taste, potassium reminds
the patient he is
very much alive
and the laugh is on him

for several days he talked
to us with hand signs
and all of us got frustrated
by the lack of understanding
our separating worlds forced
upon us

he wanted to know how long
he had been there
would he be able to talk again
and see, he pointed to each side of his mouth
biting his fingers
first on one side
and then the other
it was difficult to eat
and some jello dribbled out to
prove his point

we joked with him and his nurse
with a reminder to her to be agile
because you never know about
an instantaneous cure for
coyotes, in the meantime be sure
to come in on the right side
and stay away from the left

later, he came to me
in a dream
cleared his throat
and spoke
I was so surprised
and pleased for him
I forgot to listen
to what he was saying

I stay away
from hardline guessing
do my dreaming
in a light state
and wait for him
to tell me
a second time
for emphasis

» The Man Who Travels

The man who travels
speaks to mountains
in his region

In the north
a snow peak

In the valley
buttes above the fog

In the south
a mountain by the ocean

The man who travels
speaks to mountains
in his region

Each peak receives
and begins the journey
of the dead

And speaks of shadows
where death
is not death

And the path
from earth
is real

The man who travels
speaks to mountains
in his region

The man who
travels mountains
travels
and speaks of death

» Hands Tell

Hands tell
of stories and directions
of the wind and breathing times

Like the screech
and grinding of an earthquake
coming first by sound

The sacred fire
made in a
way of thinking
has bubbles rising
from the flame

Cover the earth
again with fire
and death show symbols
traveling in a hall

» Red Crane Coming

The coming of the
white man
was a sacred
event

Like shadow
being or
unknown
spirits

They came
strangely odd
we called
them, Red Crane

For we
knew Sandhill

Crane and
loved him

while Red Crane
was a special
being and rare

» Red Pond

Comes the morning
when the blood of dead
lay silent
floating in the
red red water

Where prancing
hoofprints creased
the edge of dreams
and ran down
unarmed people

The bodies cold
were running
northward
headless in the
snow fed waters

Mountain fed
yet blood
blood red pond
water pond
on Bloody Island

» Rabbit Crazy

Rabbit laughed and slapped his knees
Oh lord you're really something
and mouse laughed back

They were talking how rabbit
got so many girls and what it takes
to keep them happy

It must be something real good "Yeah
for a ninety year old . . ." he's saying
but he's really sixty two
which ain't bad for a rabbit

"They are from eighteen to old . . ."
He's talking of his women
I wonder who "they" are
and what he means by "old"

One time, rabbit to show
his friendship offered to
let mouse use his name
for one of rabbit's children

Mouse's wife said
she would beat him
if that happened
and mouse and rabbit laughed

They laughed as they talked
of women and babies
and what it takes to be
a crazy rabbit or a lover man

» Untitled

Death is a sure thing
patterned after seasons
and changing forms of light

If you do understand
yourself listen to
others and learn

I have been given
this lesson about
death and love

I sat beside an elder and
he introduced me to God
this is my nephew God
he was sitting up and had my hand

I still remember how nice
a day it was and how clear-eyed
and good his mind was

I sat by the bed
and listened to my uncle
introducing me to God

This is my nephew God
he was sitting up and had my hand
I want you to meet
my nephew
and I understood

» **The Universe Sings**

Spring days
and winter nights
have beautiful
flowers shining
they make themselves
visible
by whispering
in the color
of blue pollen

Their fragrances
are footprints
lightly traveling
on the milky way

Once I was given
a bracelet of
golden yellow flowers
on velvet darkness

Reenie said that
a mouse was painted
in the color of the sun
and that he danced for joy
on seeing flowers
blossom into stars
dancing across the universe
and singing,
singing, singing.

» » James Luna

James Luna is a Luiseño Indian and lives on the La Jolla Reservation in North County San Diego, California. His work as a multimedia installation and performance artist has received national attention for its commentary on the contemporary American Indian lifestyle. Writing has and continues to be an intricate part of his work in exhibit planning, dialogue for performance, and visual sketching.

» Half Indian / Half Mexican

I'm half Indian and Half Mexican.
I'm half many things.
I'm half compassionate/I'm half unfeeling.
I'm half happy/I'm half angry.
I'm half educated/I'm half ignorant.
I'm half drunk/I'm half sober.
I'm half giving/I'm half selfish.

A self made up of many things,
I do not have to be anything for anybody but myself.
I have survived long enough to find this out.
I am forty-one years old and am happy with
        my whole—self.
Don't let your children wait as long . . .

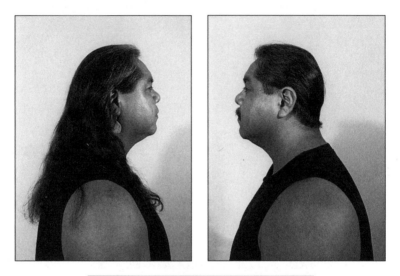

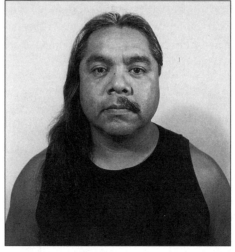

» The Artifact Piece

The burns on the fore and upper arm were sustained during days of excessive drinking. Having passed out on a campground table, trying to walk, he fell into a campfire.

Not until several days later, when the drinking ceased, was the seriousness and pain of the burn realized.

Having received a telephone call that his father had returned to the veterans hospital (where he did not recover) and having excellent feelings about a new relationship, the total impact of the news was excessively emotional.

He proceeded to drink a fifth of whiskey, fell on his face. A slight scar and a lump under the skin document the event.

Having been married less than two years, emotional scars from alcoholic family backgrounds were cause for showing fears of giving, communicating, and mistrust.

Skin callus on ring finger remains, along with assorted painful and happy memories.

Drunk beyond the point of being able to defend himself, he was jumped by people from another reservation.

After being knocked down, he was kicked in the face and upper body. Saved by an old man, he awoke with a swollen face covered with dried blood.

Thereafter he made it a point not to be as trusting among relatives and other Indians.

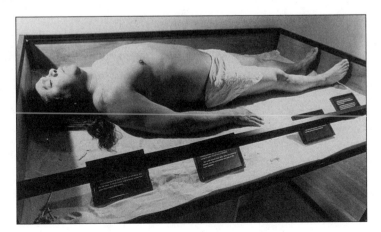

» **He's Resting Now**

The 11:30 A.M. sunlight is hot and has made everyone that more uncomfortable at graveside. Lying in the open casket, the makeup on our
friend/relation could not hide the green pallor of his skin, caused by a
rotting liver and kidneys.

The air is still except for the constant buzz of the deer flies. . . .
Summertime, the fall or whatever season, the air seems so still at burials.

The people, the tribal people, have assembled, waiting patiently for
the final rites. It is one of the few times now that the people get along; act
as a tribe; put pettiness aside; humble their ways.

This man was a veteran, and the VFW Color Guard has been invited
to pay tribute. The soldiers march—salute—stand stiff at attention. With
great care and precision, the soldier men fold the flag that has draped the
coffin into a tight triangle. The flag is presented to the nearest relation
and the commander says, "On behalf of the United States of America . . ."
The soldiers snap to attention, "Taps" is played, the sound of the trumpet
echoes through you and out to the surrounding land:

Listen . . .

Why do we Indians drink so, why do we drink ourselves to early
deaths? I heard it said that it is a hard life to be an Indian. Perhaps so,
but drinking does not make life more tolerable, just less to see and feel.
Maybe life is sometimes too easy for us, with the free programs and no
incentive projects taking our pride and strength, giving us more time
to drink.

Drinking is a part of the Indian way of life now, it is few and far between of those who it does not affect. Alcoholism comes into our home
by mother, father, brothers and sisters, aunts and uncles, grandpas and
grandmas, cousins, and friends.

After the casket is lowered into the ground, before we shovel in the
earth, each of us passes by and tosses a handful of earth as a last goodbye.
That is it, life is over, and only the memories are left.

The people say if the dead has suffered in life or dying, "He's resting now . . ."

» "The News"

> I am considered both brilliant and a fool
> in certain circles.
> I am a chronic alcoholic, artist and
> competent administrator.
> Pictures at 11:00.

» Untitled

> Passed out on Willie's sofa
> Breeze blows faded curtain in open window
> Curl up for warmth
> Ray Price Western music on the clock radio

» City Notes

In this morning the absence of the serenity of the reservation is great. It isn't as though I haven't lived in town, as all told I've spent more time here than in the mountains.

Is it the morning sounds of the sun coming over the hills, in its wake the conversations of birds and other animals or the stretching of trees, plants and grasses in the sweet smell of the sage air . . . or is it the nights that I crave?

» Mr. Anonymous

Gotta bottle at the local store—another someone buying booze. They give me the look—another of those guys.

I do not wave a badge with my credentials, feats & the like—though there are times I want to shout, "Hey god-damn-it, do you know who I am? This is not some average Joe you're selling drinks to!"

Then I recover to my senses—walk the cold sidewalk home clutching my bottle in the paper sack as if it were the Academy Award for Best Picture.

›› "How To Make An Ass Of Yourself"

1. Drink ½ gallon red wine on top of numerable preceding beers.
2. Have telephone numbers of friends that live long-distance.
3. Have a telephone.
4. They are home when you call.
5. You will not remember what you said the next day.

›› Untitled

Taste cold water from tin cup—flavor of rust coming through flaked enamel.

Mountain water tastes similar—metals eroded and washed down.

We pass friends on Hwy—going to visit one another, we pull over to the side of the road. Leaning on a car hood conversation, cold beer pulled from beneath ice of a cooler.

Beer on a good day tastes like mountain water from a tin cup.

›› Morning Reservation

Earth turns over from its sleep to face the ascending sun. Mountains with flannel blanket of snow and frost begins to vary in color tones in changing light.

Cold wet air stays consistent
Consistent stays the cold wet air

In the older reservation houses, many families have to move to the room where there is warmth; Small camps are formed around wood stoves containing glowing embers.

From stove pipes, long thin whiffs of smoke rise and disappear into the morning.

» **Untitled**

Rusted barbed wire fence.
Wet wood smell.
Blades of grass bend downward from weight of water on their backs.
Drank a little wine, looking out the window.
A little red wine.

» **"Red Shoes"**

Uncle's house had always looked seemingly uninhabited—unpainted wood exterior grey/brown, rusted nail streaks pour downward. Roof of split shingle: Big open hole in unused kitchen; Skylight, wind mouth, rain bowl . . .

Come in . . . Through wire screen door; drags when pulled open over worn smooth step. Enter from back door, front door long ago sealed shut.

Dust (musk) scented room of single man, living alone for years.

Faded sun bleached flour sack curtains, lets in cool color beneath roll shade, pulled two-thirds down. . . . Cannot see clearly in or out.

Sound of fine sand grit underneath your shoes as you walk, floor-boards creak.

Bed is neatly made; Piled high with many blankets; red wool, grandma quilt, army-issue olive green; blankets with frayed edges—soft mashed pillows.

Night table assembled with reading lamp, tobacco pipes—pipe tools, radio tuned for late-night talk programs, reading materials and useful junk.

Wall decor of calendars from various years ago with the highlight belonging to Marilyn Monroe 195?; Blond locks fall upon full breast, pink nipples point upward as ripe strawberries, white cream skin on red background blanket; Miller Highlife Beer advertisement light, of Spanish girls that parade on revolving scroll, inviting lips, tousled black hair, skirts hiked-up, showing lots of thigh; Cowboy and horse pictures complement bridle and hackamore, brittle old leather; Sweat-stained caps and western straw hats hang on headless nails, some sort of documentation.

Chairs, wall shelves piled with magazines: Western periodicals, sports, *Life & Post*, and the few "dirty" ones found at the bottom of the stacks.

Sheet functions as door for clothes closet.

The other room, the only other room, is what was the kitchen. It is now a storeroom of collectibles; A reflection of random saving—They said, "It might come in handy, save it."

In this room amongst the mess, the smell & dust, I found his old work boots—covered with a sprinkling of dried blood from his first and last hemorrhage.

» Notes: 1985
James Luna
Luiseño Indian

Sunday, July 14, 1985, 8:15 P.M.

For all intents and purposes, the most difficult and challenging areas of art for myself are those of making statements that are of clarity and simplicity.

What should be foremost in the intent of the American Indian artists is the opportunity to say, not to be spoken for or about, concerning our ways, our feelings and thoughts. It is truly unfortunate that there are so few Indian artists who address current issues of Indian communities or those of American contemporary art.

9:47 P.M.

Dear American Indian Art Patrons:

American Indian life and arts are rich with diversity, purpose and heritages. Indian arts go well beyond the images of the stoic brave atop a snarling pony, plume and beads of many colors. . . .

Fuck you sincerely

J. L.

11:30 P.M.

The truest of Indian artists are not dead—they are, though, ignored, bypassed or placed as archaeological wonder. To name but a few of these prominent positions, let us include the storytellers, the herb-gathering knowledge, the basket maker, the songs, the singers, the comic, the comedy, the spiritual leaders . . .

Monday, 1:00 A.M.

For those of us who bridge the gaps within our culture, in possession of Indian knowledge, as well as trained artists, I coin the label of "Contemporary Traditionalists."

6:15 A.M.

There are particular pieces of my art which intend the viewer to be in the realm of social conditions that are much talked about but not felt about. Indian alcohol abuse is one of the subjects I work with. This particular subject, along with Indian modern ceremony, altered everyday objects, I consider something similar to the process and action of a transformer toy: A room changed to a church; objects to people; common utensils to ceremonial objects; and videotaping to a physical place.

6:45 A.M.

Fixed breakfast for the boys, finished notes, will awake my sweetie before I leave; she has a different work schedule.

With the sun beginning to heat, the dry grasses crack, the birds and stones stir, I smile to myself with the thought that I'm in a position of doing something for the people, creating understanding . . .

» » Stephen Meadows

Stephen Meadows is a Californian of Ohlone and pioneer descent. His work has appeared in anthologies and small magazines nationwide. He devotes much of his time to public radio in the interest of raising social and political consciousness.

» John's Song

At the end of the counter
the old man's falsetto quavers
brittle as his cup
some tune from the twenties
his voice a frayed reed
or the sound of bees
nesting wood
It is his last October
Wrists about to let his hands
go the way of fruit
he does not lay them down

though they shake ever slightly
out of the sleeves
It is a song from the twenties
he moves as he sings
the way I've seen sick gulls
rocking in the wind
he does not care who watches
the white dusted fragment
of his body and the frail song mythic
and fragile as his sight

» A Fire If It Burns

Bent willows rattle
in the wind overhead
The remnant of the match
still smokes in your hand
I was twelve you were fifty
I was fifty you were twelve
Hovered over the wet wood
that barely burning symbol
of the generations passing
in the thicket near
that rumble of the river
Your eyes red as firelight
from drinking all the beers
the white man's curse upon each
swimming that rare blood
with the roar of the wind
and water in the trees
you stared across that fifty
years the wild eyes rough
as the stubble on your jaw
the despair planted then
on the full of drift river
comes home every Christmas

everlasting
like that other kind of gift

» **In the Shadow of the Tower**

In the quiet
your photo is upon me
you are fond of this setting
the mission adobe
where they murdered our people
in the name of a merciful god
It is history you tell me
your daughters now drink
from the same cup
take names from their water
You have taken their story
as your own
You have lived their religion
Your children grow up
in the shadow of the tower
where the bells of the fathers
rang bodies into the fields
In your eyes in the photo
that sadness gapes open
like the mouths of those
dead ones you cannot but witness
looking out from that bleak place
unknowing and imprisoned in the dark

» **Blues For Juanito**

No amenities but cheap wine
and those fits of weeping
the distempered wet look
of some dog and the black
cast stove picked up red hot

with a couple of burlap sacks
thrown smoking on the truck
when they moved you
to the corn crib shack

Son of old Manuel
far down on the ladder
of the children
it was always you and your brother
and the drunks from town
in the beaten old cars that limped
through the summer dust
and shimmered in the heat
near the river

When you died on county sheets
of TB and too much wine
no more the soiled blanket
the broken cot crying
to yellow heaven in the heat
the few windows cracked
the lantern too
cracked
and remaining the tin shack
that rats couldn't climb
the bad sawhorse leaning
and the white alder
dead in the blackberry vines
like bone

»   The Intrusion

The furred hood of morning
crowds close about the house
Down the canyon it is silent
as time before sound
White trunks of birches
dismember the darkness

from streambed to cabin
in this bell jar of woodland
the snow moving in from the brushline
waits cold at the door

» Grass Valley

The dirt is red here
stone speckles the ground
a light snow has fallen
in the night
the room smells of matches
her husband is dying
she splits up the wood
in her bathrobe
morning by morning
releasing the days

» For My Father Having Lost His Mind

Madrone trees knotted
above dry yellow grass
the wind down the valley
in the woods genuflecting
red limbs moving against
the hard high scope of the mountain
you sit in this thicket
speechless
amazed
your white hair disheveled
your mind a great room
where the same bit of music
strains above the sound of the wind
in the undulating branches

you hear the same music
again and again

it is the same wind you knew
half a century ago
the same sun poised
above the notch in the mountain
and the same boy waiting
in the corn
in the wind
for the night to come on
all the slow walk home
to the one light for miles
and that solace

» For Chief Joseph

Your cook fires here
just a short time ago
you passed without sound
by this stream in the dark
the smoke now in tatters
in the dawn wind unfurling
like the death
in bad blankets
of your merciful wisdom
the blue world you worshipped
now follows you solemn
as a grave

» The Dying Place

You are herded
to a meal
you've forgotten
how to swallow

The white caps
of nurses

are curt
among the wheelchairs

The grey heads
are tilted like blossoms
in a memory garden
each to its own sun

» Bare-Root

I planted the apricot
near an old peach
at the edge of this storm
that exhausts a worn month
placing the roots
into the earth just so
as if each had a predestined place
a warm sleeve in the soil

To allay these fears
that crowd close
in this dark
I revere now at all cost
the slow desperate days
toward the spring
that pull hope
out of the bark

» The Spirit of the Bayonet

You feel your feet
ride the dream
firm over the ground
you see only the tip of it
flash out in front of you
obscene and ancient
as the cruelty of war

the blue steel ahead
is an animal star
that glistens like death
over the hovel
of the world
the hands are precision
in this manner of worship
the aggravated ritual
of self abnegation
eyes pouring hot
upon the cold point
impaling the red air

» Suicide Creek

Above Suicide Creek
the trees felled
one by one
can be heard to scream
The ridge clear cut
the sound of them falling
the wood at the last
joined place
twisting back upon itself

Where the first sun
hits the alders
the drone of the chain saws
the broken fir swept before
giant yellow cats
already at six

» At the Crossing

A chainsaw dismembers the silence
of a white afternoon

in a pasture
the crackle of fires
in pruned orchard wood

little to do midwinter
but cut and burn brush

drink warm booze
in long sleeves

and watch the smoke
crossing the river
enter in among the trees

» For the Living

Standing high on this hillside
the wind off the Pacific
forming the language of grasses
and escarpment eternally speaking
the sea birds far out
on their planes of air
gather and squander
what the short days encompass
We make what we can
of what reason can give us
we take from these all too brief moments
some reckoning of meaning
hoping as we hurtle haphazard
through this storm of a cosmos
to make some small imprint
while the birds in their white realm
reeling over the tumbling green ocean

this plated earth gliding
beneath us like a wind
under shoulders
and the language we hear
in the grass on this hillside
is all of it mythic and wondrous
as the Goddesses dream

» » William Oandasan

William Oandasan was a member of the Tano'm branch of the Yuki (Ukommo'm), who have been living in Round Valley of northern California for ten thousand years. He received a bachelor's degree from the University of California at Santa Cruz, and while earning two graduate degrees, he wrote three books of poetry: *A Branch of California Redwood*, *Moving Inland*, and *Round Valley Songs* (which won the American Book Award in 1985). His most recent works are *A Yukian Bibliography* and *North of San Francisco*. He died on September 17, 1992.

» Grandmothers Land

around the house stood an
orchard of plum, apple and pear
a black walnut tree, one white pine,
groves of white oak and willow clumps
the home of Jessie was largely redwood

blood, flesh and bone sprouted
inside her womb of redwood
for five generations
the trees now stand unpruned and wild

after spreading to the four directions
the seeds of Jessie have returned
afternoon sunlight on the field
breezes moving grass and leaves
memories with family names wait
within the earth, the mountains,
the valley, the field, the trees

» Round Valley Songs

I

song gives birth to
the story and dance
as the dance steps
the story speaks

from heart through mind into image:
the pulse of the four directions
the voice of our blood
the spirit of breath and words

in chipped and tattered
weavings of a willow basket
the voice of an ancient age
dreaming of breath

from fresh currents of night air
above manzanitas near the cemetery
the words of ancient lips
turn in our blood again

long ago black bears
sang around our lodge fires

tonight they dance
alive through our dreams

an emptied bottle of Coors
ditched in moonlight at Inspiration Point
mirrors the faces of drunkards
cold like snow

on the summit of Blue Nose
night wind races through long hair
and tears stream down laughing Yuki faces
tens of thousands of years old

in print for People's use:
the songs of the old ways
the words of ancient lips
the spirit of breath and words

may the rich brown clay, the feather
and foam, the marrow of our ways,
not be the ash of memory in print
but cold mountain water

» Round Valley Songs

II

1

the blackberry grows sweet,
plump and juicy near Williams Creek
it bloomed thousands of years ago
when we savored its flavor first

2

home sleeps 1,000 miles northwest
when I palm the green soapstone
from the stream east of Aunt Mary's
smells of redwood surface again

3

near the foot of slopes fenc-
ing the valley on the north
the reservation rests quietly
like resistance burned out

4

through the heart of Covelo
Commercial Boulevard parades past
a gas station, cafe, saloon, store, old barn
signs of the empire

5

an emptied bottle of Coors
ditched in moonlight at Inspiration Point
mirrors the faces of drunkards
cold like snow

6

across the street nearly mute
an old woman moans alone
inside the Buckhorn saloon
cowboys stomp and drink up

7

in brilliant feathers and strength
three Filipino gaming cocks
appear from across the water
in the yard pullets cluck excitedly

8

west by east, north from south
one historical line cuts
apart the valley's lives
sharp like bloodlines

9

across the salty distance
and decades of grief since Hiroshima

the shadows of holocaust hang
over the valley and earth

10

next to the road into Covelo
Mr. White's land lies for desire,
greed, deceit, shame, alcohol, distrust
all's now forgotten though not forgiven

11

between the round piece of green soapstone
and my firm touch
Medicine Hill so far away,
a horizon-line at dawn

12

Turner Creek's the core of winter
but blackberry buds flare again
and transform the light of spring
fire enough for another year

» Natural Law

Deep in the shade
Of the forest, a hunter,
Armed for survival,
And the victim, an old bear . . .
He chews bits of bark,
Taking a step at a time,
Upwind, twenty steps from her,
Unaware of the plot. She
Positions her piece, taking aim,
Centering on the heart.
Her finger slides
To the trigger, slowly tensing
To spring the lever.
No one will witness
This killing but trees,

Grass and insects locked
In their own struggles.
Even nature lies
As if asleep,
Powerless in making
A quick end of it
As it is in preventing one.
The light of life,
High above the drama,
Shines on.

» Hunger

So here I am,
Having gone to the shore
Of the powerful
And uncontrollable

For a taste of freedom

And finding a paved path
With safety signs.

I feel humiliation
Turn to frustration,
Then anger
Become a little red
Sign.

I break from the path

And kick the sign
Off the cliff.

As I perch
With the front halves
Of my feet over
The ledge,
Hunched with my knees
Tucked under my chin,

I savor the salt air,
The night of waves,
The weight of the sea.

» Laguna Landscape

Just off bleak and deadly
Speedways, beyond sight
And sound of train,
Truck and airplane,
The changeless earth
Today's rustic searches for
Waits in cliffs of red rock.
Many times the heartless
Sun and wind have turned
The poor rustic back
To Albuquerque.
Still persons whose lives
Span more generations
Than Interstate 40 has years
On the soil of this
Arid place, they know
The land
Unfolding from the eye
Toward red cliffs
Set in the stillness
Of silence.

» Acoma

For many distant travelers
The way to Acoma is merely
Interstate 40,
A four-lane sear
Of asphalt
Stitched in between wire
Fences and telephone lines,

Running like a scar
Across the flesh
Of an ancient landscape;
They almost never know
The old way south by north
Where you can fly today
From a uranium stripmine
To the sacred city
Standing on top
White Rock Mesa.
Corn and rituals predate
The Christian mission there
Like a breathing shrine,
And the way to Acoma for many
Is a place for curious pottery.
Or a refreshment stop.
But for those who still
Travel the four directions,
The way to Acoma
Is always the way.

» » Wendy Rose

Wendy Rose was born in Oakland, California, in 1948. Her tribal affiliations are Hopi and Miwok. She has been the coordinator and an instructor of American Indian Studies at Fresno City College since 1984 and is the author of twelve volumes of poetry, three of which are in press. Her most recent collection is *Bone Dance: New and Selected Poems, 1965—1993* (forthcoming from the University of Arizona Press).

» We Live!
For Indians of All Tribes
Alcatraz Island 1979 / New York City 1978

> We live!
> in deep places
> where shadows glide
> on canyon walls
> wings out, tips up,
> circling down

to textbook pages
dyed with our blood,
red and wet
from the slip
of white tongues;
in museums
our bones exposed
to weep and howl
to clatter helplessly
clutter the halls
learning to be fossils
learning not to see
the future;
alone and apart
hungry for a final storm
rain impending
and teeth of wolves
fast and lean,
tremble of rabbits
watchful and fat;
We live! in our dance
our slow walk
our run to new visions
historical re-visions
water of fingertips
touching, eyes embracing;
in our communities
our villages, one Village,
ourselves, our unborn,
our twice-born, our never-born
in who we still are
for ourselves
for all our relations
for who we will be
Chahtah Dineh Hopituh Haudenosaunee
Lakota Inuit Nim Anishinabe
We live! kneeling

by secret fires
stones of sweat lodge
hiss of living breath,
sunrise from hogan door,
smoke in trees from painted tipis,
heavy perfume of cedar lodge,
earth-baked musk of dark pueblo,
leaves on ancient Longhouse floor,
hot waxy mist of iglu,
pandanus hut of rain forest
crowded in solitude
unified at last
We live!
in concentration camps, tourist centers,
museums, real-live-Indian-villages,
reservations, rancherias, colonies,
cities, suburban fields, ivory towers;
radio stations, laboratories, satellites,
mountains of microwave towers;
gourds rattle, flutes breathe,
wood and rawhide pulse
soles of feet become hoof and paw
to shuffle and beat
upon the earth and from within
an answering thunder
throats sing
down the rain, up the sun,
up the corn, up the melons,
up the daughters and sons
holding to what is sacred,
holding to what is left,
making it new—how old it is!
holding the land holding the rivers
holding turquoise sky holding holy mountain
holding the earth holding the bones
holding the bones holding the bones
holding the bones

» For the Scholar Who Wrote a Book About the "American Indian Literary Renaissance"

It was winter. We were not loved.
We had nothing but our weapons
loose and easy. The enemy
could be anywhere, was actually
everywhere. Our hands were stiff.
Our lungs were hot. We carried
sacred fire. We camped behind you.
You were blind. So we laughed.

                    Do you remember
when you twisted the wax
from your ears
              and shouted to me
"You finally speak!"
because now you
could finally hear?

The renaissance, you said, had begun
and beads began to sprout around our necks,
stones germinated from the backs of our fingers;
the drum began in the middle of the night
and you said "The words have broken free at last
from those silent stoic teeth"

and from the pain
of forgetting
we almost agreed.

When you turned around
your mouth a great O
was it that you finally heard
our long and noisy wait for you?
Or did you only hear
mosquito squeal into your ear?

» Trophy in Two Acts

In a television documentary a scientist explained how he obtained
a section of schoolhouse wall in Hiroshima after the atomic explosion
in 1945.

See where my finger is? this white line
across the center—oh, two feet square or so—
the flash mark shows it went off
exactly where we wanted, level and force
precisely foretold, smoothly predicted.
I brought this home to show everyone.
It satisfied the feds, fascinated the kids,
so I kept it on my mantle then on my desk
at the university.
Good old Yankee know-how is the way of the future,
I tell my students

> You lazy boy, get up! See,
> the sky pales over the hill
> and the happy sun will pull you from bed
> by your feet! Your breakfast is cooked;
> come and eat now. All your clothes
> are laid out. Your books wait, little scholar,
> in the new red bag you chose in the store.

I picked it up myself. I was there.
You should have seen my boy's face!
Did you see any dead bodies? he shouted.
Was there blood? Son,
I stepped among the skulls,
yellowing bones, blackened bones,
bones by the millions. I counted.
I measured. I judged our success.
Technology is the way of the future,
I told him. And he said
Boy, you sure got those Japs!

a moment more you sleep
and I take this moment for my own.
I am watching you as I often do
a kiss so light you will dream
a moth has landed on your cheek.
I see them in the streets
refugees from burning homes.
How lucky you are! walking past them
to your lessons. How lucky
that our city was not hit!

Open 'er up and drop 'er!
This is only bloodless surgery,
excising of a tumor, burning
of a paper mountain and paper people,
dissolution of useless toys;
if I were Truman I would have dropped
a dozen more.

Mama, did you see where I put my cap?
It hurts when you comb my hair and anyway
I'm too big. Today we go on a field trip
to see an artist at work. No, I'm not hungry.
I'll eat later!

How clever we are. You know, I predicted it,
worked the calculations even in my sleep,
my short little sleep cool enough to need a blanket.
It was my own work. I published it.
I named it. I gave it a baptism of fire.
The honor is mine. We are the American pride,
gratified boys at play in the sky.
We stopped Hitler, we ended the genocide,
we joined the nations together.
I brought this home to show you
what your daddy does for a living.

If once more I could see you
start to school, flesh of my burning flesh,

child forming in my eyes. *Newborn again*
you would mouth my melting breast,
make bird sounds in your sleep,
dream in the crook of my arm.
I must touch you again,
my fingers flowing into you
and you back to me, music
in your flaming hair,
crackle and spit
of your high singing voice
returned within, growing bigger . . .

. . . with morning
a light has come.

» **For the Campus Committee on the Quality of Life**

For the campus committee on the Quality of Life that proposed
organizing coffee hours and bowling teams while my students have sickle
cell crises in emergency rooms where doctors refuse to touch them, find
rocks thrown at their mixed-blood kids, find themselves living too close
to the cowboy-teen-KKK, lose hope when their mother dies from having
too little money to fix her broken Hmong heart, drop out of nursing
school because the feds define "Indian" differently this year, discover that
their wives were sterilized without their knowledge merely for crossing
a border, try not to listen to evangelists who preach love with NRA cards
in their hands and pro-lifers screaming for executions and war, try not to
drink tonight, bundle up the babies in an unheated garage and wait for
the BIA check that failed to bounce down from Sacramento. . . .

> . . . we have stripped ourselves bare for you
> and you eat, eat, just that simple thing
> unable to taste the blood or feel against your teeth
> the bone, along your palate the stretch and snap
> of arteries

> > or have you scraped
> > the bumps from your tongue

that would tell you the kind
of taste we are, sweet
or bitter, when without thinking
you chew us up and watch TV,
read scripture, relax
into the suburban night,
turn up the dry breath
of your air conditioner.

O we are the bones
a forest of bones
stream beds and boulders
of bones, we are the bones
of the gold, earth brown bones,
bones of clay, obsidian, redwood bones,
mescal bones, bones that are hollow,
weak and hurting bones, bones you give
to your mutt in the morning,
bridges of bones, fences, horizons, barriers
of bones, planets of bones,
bone prisons, bone colleges, encampments,
here and there of bones, we are the bones,
the bones of what you try to forget

the bones of what you think are just lies
the bones that stop you from feeling good
the bones that follow you home
the bones that dust your dreams at night
before they
float away.

» For the Angry White Student Who Wanted to Know If I Thought White People Ever Did Anything Good for 'the Indians'

O yes I told her.
First of all
there's Häagen-Dazs

though
we had to supply
the flavors
and Siberians learned
to freeze it.
          I would not
          forget
          the wheat and raisins
          for cinnamon rolls,
the English dough
into which
is put
our sweet potato
or pumpkin sauce,
whipped cream on top
from tough Highland cows.
          And bluejeans are good
though it was
our cotton they used

with staple long enough
to be spun and dyed
with indigo from India.
          And the horse
          was a good thing
          I like horses
big enough to pull
the tipi poles,
drag travois across
the cratered plain
so punched with holes
that wheels bog down.
          And coffee, canned peaches,
          oranges and sugar
from reeds selected and cut
by our sea—going cousins
          and melons
          so like our gourds

> but soft and sweet,
the oasis
within August.
> Computers, boots, baroque music,
> paper more fragile than birch
to replace Mayan books burned
by Spanish tantrums.
> Typewriters, trucks, rock 'n' roll,
> electric lights, polished steel
for the knife and the ax. And guns, outboard motors,
customers
willing to be silent
as we auction off the days
remaining.

» The Endangered Roots of a Person

I remember lying awake
in a Phoenix motel. Like that
I remember coming apart accidentally
like an isolated hunk of campfire soot
cornered by time into a cave.
I live even now
in an archaeological way.

> Becoming strong on this earth is a lesson
> in not floating, in becoming less transparent,
> in becoming an animal shape against the sky.

We were born
to lose our eyes in the Sun Dance
and send out lengths of fishline
for the clouds, reel them in
and smooth away all the droughts
of the world.

> Sometimes Medicine People shake their hands
> over you and it is this; to drop your bones

into the sand, to view yourself
bursting through the city
like a brown flash flood.
The healing of the roots
is that thunderhead-reeling;
they change and pale
but they are not in danger now.

That same morning
I went for coffee down the street
and held it, blowing dreams
through the steam, watching silver words
bead up on my skin. The Hand-trembler said
I belong here. I fit in this world
as the red porcelain mug
merges in the heat of my hand.

On some future dig
they'll find me like this
uncovered where I knelt
piecing together the flesh
that was scattered in the mesa wind
at my twisted-twin birth.

» If I Am Too Brown or Too White for You

remember I am a garnet woman
whirling into precision
as a crystal arithmetic
or a cluster and so

why the dream
in my mouth,
the flutter of blackbirds
at my wrists?

In the morning
there you are

at the edge of the river
on one knee

and you are selecting me
from among polished stones
more definitely red or white
between which tiny serpents swim

and you see
that my body is blood
frozen into giving birth
over and over, a single motion,

and you touch the matrix
shattered in winter
and begin to piece together
the shape of me

wanting the curl in your palm
to be perfect
and the image less clouded,
less mixed

but you always see
just in time
working me around
the last hour of the day

there is a small light
in the smoke, a tiny sun
in the blood, so deep
it is there and not there,

so pure
it is singing.

» **Moths Point the Way to Oklahoma**

East of Amarillo
we ride astride

the continent
on the whirling black feet
of the red Ford.
Your ochre plain
sweeps beneath
summer's first flood
rushing west
to tease down a tornado
from the smoky sky.
In every direction
we dance and with us
spin the great moths
rolling their tongues
into roadside foxglove
as we raise impure water
to our lips, hold onto
one another tight, end up
covered with the finest
dust.

» **April Daughtersong**
Coarsegold 1993

ancestor dream me dead
dream me dream me
dead daughter
only in the abstract
flicker of pollen
useless on rock
dream me dead
unplug my ears
keep singing
give me dreams
but dream me dead
daughter only
in the abstract

unplug my ears
keep singing I smoke and sit
daughter only in the abstract
pray for years, wait for bones
to stiffen gleam opaline
listen and wait, lean
along granite cracks
break inside asphalt
endure the drought
and wait daughter
only in the abstract
fear dreams that flood
into the heart escape
where arteries wheeze
pump the blood dry
spiral of dust
on city sidewalk small
gray feather still
attached to sinew
behind honeysuckle bush stubborn
or stupid pine cone
on uppermost branch
of long-dead tree mountain side
agape with quarry scar
wounded one ancestor dream
me dead daughter only
in the abstract descendant
who seeps unseen
into how things are

» » Georgiana Valoyce-Sanchez

Georgiana Valoyce-Sanchez is Chumash and O'odham (Tohono/Pima), and is a recognized member of the Coastal Band of the Chumash Nation. She was born and raised in California and currently teaches American Indian literature and Native American women's literature at California State University at Long Beach. She is one of fifteen faculty members of various disciplines who are reading the latest works on Christopher Columbus in order to discuss the consequences of the encounter. Her latest publications include *Invocation: L.A.*, an anthology of "multi-cultural" poetry that won the American Book Award in 1990, and *Daily Guideposts 1991*, a collection of daily devotionals by inspirational writers. She recently completed the poetry manuscript *A Light To Do Shellwork By*, which is dedicated to her father, a respected Chumash elder who died on August 15, 1991.

» A Light To Do Shellwork By

One day
      all of life catapulted into one
day   one moment
of sunlight

filtering through a high bedroom window
framed by blue curtains
filtering through the waiting
of the grownups
        sunlight
and the laughter of children outside
warming my father's
dying

My father turns his head to acknowledge the sun
        The light   the light
            he says
                    and the light within

            It's a good light to do shellwork by

The ocean sang in my father's hands
abalone pendants shimmered rainbows
from the ears of pretty girls

and shellwork dotted driftwood carvings
        cowrie shells, cone shells, volute shells
        red, black, white, blue, brown, green shells
the life they once held
sacred
old stories etched on
the lifeline of my father's palm

I hold my father's hand
my own shellwork words
my poet's eyes noting the light
        how through the bedroom door
the ears of fresh white corn piled
on the kitchen table
harvest the afternoon sun
        how it shines through a glass of water
touches
my mother's white hair as she leans
to embrace my father
        the hush of twilight

and how the sunset
like a trail of wild lupines
or the tracings on seashells
tells stories
of our origin
as it lights up the sky
with fire

» The Eye of the Flute

Enter the eye

From the north
a ribbon of geese drifts
high above the earth

      far below

beside a weathered wood shack
in the spring green foothills
of distant blue mountains
an old man sits
polishing stone

      Dogs bark in the distance

Down the hill a brown horse
black mane flying
runs along the reservation road
and three children and their mother
stand beside a fence
watching

      Beyond the fence a rusty tractor

sits fallow in the field
silent as the man beside it
watching the horse
run free

The eye watches   the eye

sees   the image
held
to still-point

Silence

Silence that holds all songs
that holds the breath
to play all songs
to life

hush

listen to the music

The horse is running still
hoofbeats on pavement a drum
black mane flying
free
within the still-point
of the song
        the locus of the poem
the eye of the flute

Three children and their mother
stand beside a fence
their father close by
all watching
the horse run free

Dogs bark in the distance

An old man holds a polished stone
up to the sun
turning it
to catch the light

High above the earth
a ribbon of geese drifts south
the call of a long journey
echoing
across the endless sky

» The Dolphin Walking Stick

He says
sure you look for your Spirit
symbol   your totem
only it's more a waiting
watching
for its coming

You listen
You listen for the way it
feels   deep inside

Sometimes something comes
that feels   almost
right
the way that swordfish
kept cropping up with
its long nose

but no
and so   you wait
knowing it is getting
closer   knowing
it is coming

And when that dolphin
jumped out of the water
its silver blue sides all shiny
and glistening with rainbows
against the white cloud sky
and the ocean so big
and deep
it went on
forever
I knew it had come

My father rests his hand upon
the dolphin's back
the dolphin's gaze serene

above the rainbow band
wrapped around the walking stick

He leans upon his brother friend
and walks across the room

    As he walks
strings of seashells clack softly
like when ocean waves tumble
rocks and shells and
the gentle clacking song
follows each wave

as it pulls back into
the sea

    The sea

    So long ago
The Channel Islands filled
with Chumash People like
colonies of sea lions
along the shore so many
people
it was time for some to
make the move
across the ocean to
the mainland

Kakunupmawa the sun
the Great Mystery
according to men's ideas
said
        don't worry
I will make you a bridge
the rainbow
will be your bridge only
don't look down
or you will fall
Have Faith

So the chosen ones began
the long walk across
the rainbow
they kept their eye straight
toward where the mainland was
and all around them
was the ocean sparkling
like a million scattered crystals
so blue-green and singing
lovely and cool
some looked down
and fell
into the deep
to become
the dolphins
they too
the People

My father turns to look at me

Someone told me that story
long before I ever heard it
It's those old ones
he says pointing up to the ceiling
as if it were sky

They sent the dolphin to me

I always loved the sea

» Chumash Man

"Shoo-mash," he says
and when he says it
I think of ancient sea lion hunts
and salt spray windswept
across my face

They tell him
his people are dead
"Terminated"
>   It's official
>   U.S. rubber-stamped official
>   *Chumash: Terminated*
>   a People who died
>   they say
>   a case for the anthropologists

Ah, but this old one
this old one whose face is
ancient prayers come to rest
this old one knows
who he is

"Shoo-mash," he says
and somewhere sea lions still gather
along the California coast
and salt spray
rises
rainbow mist
above the constant breaking
of the waves

» I Saw My Father Today

I saw my father today;
He lives just across town
but I'm so busy
and what with one thing
and the other
it's hard sometimes.

>   My father's face still holds
>   its tribal memory: aged oak
>   and ancient Acorn Gathering Songs.
>   A prayer, really.

It had rained for nine days.
Everything was washed to wilting,
like me after a good cry or cussing.
So we sat in his backyard
making the most of the sun.

Little birds and paper skittered
across the cracked cement. I
strummed my guitar, singing softly
as he sorted seashells and beads.

My father can't hear so well
so when I sang he sang, too, a
different tune—something old.
We sounded real good, you know?
Sort of made up our own song.

» Cahuilla Bird Song

Shadows waver in the fire's light

The gourd rattle holds a faithful rhythm
holds the old Wanikik men
and their song
holds the time
and the dance
constant
        reminding

Sometimes, children dance, too
warming to the fire
in the dark night
warming to the song
telling the ancient story
with their dance

        The birds, you see, left home
        They went to a land of
        much food   paradise

            until the freeze came
killing

Survivors told of knowing
now   about home
Down the hill the freeway
snakes through the ancient land
indifferent   mindless
of the bird's song
its fast promise like the
sound of distant water
running beyond
the next dark hill

» **Fat of the Land**

Walking to public school
beyond the housing project compound
I would ponder the "fat
of the land"
What it meant
Why my folks always talked
about it

When there was nothing left to eat
but beans   Steinbeck
would appear at our table
blowing smoke rings with his big
cigar and he'd lean back in our
rickety kitchen chair and talk
about the "fat
of the land"

When I got older with babies and
two cars in my suburban garage
my folks went back home
to Indian land
Reservation   rocks

broken bottle glass
an old shack in the foothills
of the San Gorgonios
    and I asked them
is this it Is this
It?
Where's the fat?
And my father would lean back against
a scrawny birch   blow smoke rings
with his clay pipe   and smile

I had to admit
the handful of pale pink strawberries
he had coaxed from the stony ground
were the   sweetest
I had ever tasted
and there was no denying
the singing that took place
when my mother and father knelt
to pat the earth
beneath the bare peach tree

» Mama's Water Story

My Papago Pima mama
is round and brown
like a clay water-olla
nourishing
giving us life

Mama would tell us about
the clay water-olla
how it would sit beneath
the shade of the ramada
about the hot desert sun
and how she would dip
the gourd into the

cool water
to drink

Imagine
        she would say
as we gathered around her
long ago
in that city kitchen
        Close your eyes
Imagine

She would fill a large pan
with tap water
and we would dip our
bowls as gourds
into the water
to drink
        and as we savored the water
she hinted at the taste
of wet clay
and told us of the water-soaked
edges of the gourd dipper
and how she loved to bite
into the gourd despite
Gramma's scolding

We drank deeply
tasting the gourd and wet clay
feeling the distant ancient land
beneath our bare feet
feeling the hot sun
and relentless desert beyond
the shade of the ramada
knowing
that water
        was life

In those growing-up years
of strawberry Kool Aid

and ice-cold Coca Cola
we learned to love
the taste of
water

» Petroglyphs

There are petroglyphs on caves hidden in the mountains above Santa
Barbara that tell of a people who radiated light and danced to the rhythms
of moon and sun, people who brought the stars down to earth in ritual
and sang stories of a time when all living things spoke the same language.
Deer fly across domed roofs. Dolphins swim on rock. People walk across
rainbows. Now people walk miles and climb impossible inclines to
reach the caves. But many caves are caged now, and people have to reach
through steel bars to touch the timeless air—as if it could be caged—and
they try to read the petroglyphs for some clue, some message, hoping to
decipher the language that comes to them only in dreams.

» The Dreaming

My 93-year-old father fumbles
beneath the bed
for his hunting rifle
gropes in his blindness
dreaming
he is in the Persian Gulf
needing to protect
my mother
who pleads for him
to wake

We talk him home
home
to the waking dream
of his old age
the marrow of his dreams

sucked nearly dry
and pain contorts his face
as he inches across the carpet
with hands outstretched
like a toddler
learning to walk
Awake
he smokes and dreams
of all he needs to do
before he dies
paintings his blind eyes
can see   colors
and textures
in detail   paintings
he promised to
finish   his waking
dream an anxious tug at
consciousness shaping
the real
from the dream

Each child comes from the womb
dreaming   like my father
dreaming this life
into the next
          Curled like a fetal child
beneath the blue star quilt
he tries to sleep
again   afraid
to leave
the waking world unsure
if he is entering the dream
or leaving it

My mother smoothes his hair
and talks to him
talks him to the dreaming place
he came from

telling him the war is over
and she is safe
and how tomorrow they will
sit out by the pier
and watch the boats
sail out to sea
and no matter what
everything
will be
all right

» Summer 1945

Summer   1945
Rural East L. A.
The hills   a gathering
of golden quail   waiting
uncut fields of hay swaying
in the wind around
my Japanese schoolhouse
home
          abandoned   they said
the wood frame schoolhouse
mostly one large room with
open wide windows beneath
a gently curving roof
          simple lines
a Japanese painting in
the morning mist

That summer
we lived in one side
of the schoolhouse
long   lazy days   playing
on the wide front porch
shaded by pepper trees

and I was too young to
question   where
all the children
had gone

At night
coyotes howled
and far   far away
bombs fell on Japan and
the whole world was screaming
bodies gutted   mutilated
arms and legs and heads
torn   blown apart
survivors wishing they had
died   not knowing
that soon
a new bomb would fall
and they
would lift their faces
to relatives falling
in black rain
          and I slept peacefully
safe
under a warm quilt
beside my sisters
the hum of our parents' voices
as warm as the wood stove
Mama cooked on

And the day
the bleating wave of sheep
swept
down the hill
like a flash-flood
rumbling towards
the schoolhouse
no matter the black dog
          barking at them

no matter the old man
    in the dusty brown hat
    and stick
    poking them
no matter the shouts
    and running to make them swerve
    aside
they came
    pouring through the open windows
    through the doorway
    bumping and trampling
    each other in the playroom
    milling and crying
    trying to escape their
    confinement
and the Japanese schoolhouse
shook   with their awful
confusion
the wood creaking
and moaning
like an accompaniment to
a Kabuki tragedy
    and I was afraid
in my safe side of the house
    even as they spilled
over the windows and porch
and out onto the dirt road and
they were only a dust cloud
rising
in the distance

» Confessions of an American Indian Parochial-School Teacher

It was a different rhythm I'd entered rose-bordered
    altar-cloth
clean

halls that echoed Latin chants
and though I doused myself in holy water
I was still unsure of my Carmelite glide

I worked on my glide
a turn of the head
my smile just so
hands clasped gently together
            I bought sensible shoes

We prayed on time there
small blocks of prayer
our eyes on the clock
            Hail Mary
            Holy Mary
Richard asked if a gorilla could
mate with a woman
            Pray for us

And Jesus stayed hidden in the closet
with the softball and bat

I ran all day
sand pulling at my legs
At night I dreamed of the desert
in bloom and the eagle
high above the earth
gliding

Of course I told the children that
George Washington and Custer were not
the First Americans
and how all the buffalo were slaughtered
and it was a miracle my grandmother was
even born

And all the time I was telling
I couldn't keep my eyes off the
open field outside

So I stayed   but just a little longer
blowing fire into the prayer-blocks
and leading the children outside
to the cool grass
where we sat in a circle
singing Indian songs to God

I never did perfect my Carmelite glide

» » **Greg Sarris**

Greg Sarris is a California Indian of mixed-blood ancestry—Coast Miwok, Kashaya Pomo, and Filipino on his father's side, and Jewish, German, and Irish on his mother's. He is the author of *Keeping Slug Woman Alive*, and the forthcoming *Mabel McKay: American Genius* and *Grand Avenue*, a collection of short stories. Sarris is currently an associate professor of English at the University of California at Los Angeles.

» **Sam Toms' Last Song**

The day Sam Toms turned one hundred he woke with a woman on his mind and a plan for a new life. He rubbed his eyes and looked up from the sagging bed to the light coming through the torn cardboard over the window. Six o'clock, he thought. He straightened his arms and stretched his legs. These weren't the times he could spring out of bed and walk tall through the day, even after a night of carousing or who-knows-what. That boundless strength was gone. But he had his songs, and as he watched the morning light in long rays across the room he had all the feeling of the old days, because at least today he would sing.

The woman was Nellie James. She was a distant cousin of some sort who lived just around the corner in the neatest house in the neighborhood. Red roses climbing the picket fence. Dahlias of all colors. Pink and white hollyhocks tall as a man. Golden poppies lining the pebble walkway to the front porch. The path to heaven. And inside, more flowers: African violets, pink and lavender, in the windows, on end tables. The smell of home cooking, chili and frybread, and the soft couch where he lay when she rested her hand on his heart.

He would lie on that couch again. He would eat her cooking. He would pack his suitcase today and move in. That was the plan.

He listened for Linda, his great-great-granddaughter, in the front room. Nothing. Not a sign of anyone. Not her long, gasping breathing. None of her friends. Out again all night. But it didn't matter now. Toms saw the rays of light across the room like bars he could grab onto and hoist himself to his feet. Today he would do things by himself. Tomorrow it wouldn't matter.

On the count of three he rolled himself up so he was sitting, his feet touching the floor. He reached for his oakwood cane by the nightstand, but his hand landed on the naked lamp bulb there. I can see perfectly fine, he reminded himself and slowly turned so he could see the cane. "There, there," he said, taking the cane and bracing himself. Then he pushed himself to his feet and waited, holding fast to the cane, while the room steadied itself and blood entered his legs. He looked beyond his ample stomach that showed through the open pajama top to his boxer shorts that were white with tiny red hearts. He didn't wet the bed, and as he moved for the bathroom, he could tell he was swollen like a young man. "There, there," he said again.

He decided he should have his usual bowl of Cheerios with a banana, and an extra cup of coffee. A little pep-up. Heck with the blood pressure. What do white doctors know? Sam Toms was an Indian and a hundred years old. Then he thought of his songs. He wanted to warm up, wake that cricket in his throat, as the old-timers said. But now Toms was already in the kitchen, and he figured he would eat first.

He didn't need to fast or sweat. No special foods. His songs were the kind you could buy or sell like wine during Prohibition. Use them when and how you wanted. Just don't tell where you got them, and if you're selling, don't expect to get them back. Gambling songs. Love songs. Songs

for luck. Toms bought them from dying old men and women who were
selling at a bargain. He'd sung them day in and day out years ago when-
ever he found himself in a pinch, when he needed more than the eye
could see and the hand could hold. The exact status of a down-turned
card. The heart of a woman. Now, after all this time, he was singing again.

He got busy with breakfast, reaching for this and that, peeling and
cutting, opening the rattling refrigerator, and, yes, remembering to turn
off the stove after he boiled water for coffee. When he sat down at the
scuffed Formica table with his coffee and Cheerios all on a place mat with
silverware and a napkin, he thought again of Linda. He wished she would
walk in. Surprise, he didn't need her, and wouldn't she rant and rave
when he walked out in his black suit with a suitcase in his hand. No more
two hundred and thirty-nine Social Security dollars a month to take care
of him. Never mind where he was going.

No way to treat a man who won out a century. Father of half a dozen
families. Grandfather to four times that many. Old man Toms who logged
the redwoods, built roads where there was nothing but horse trails. Who
had enough song power to pass those drunks in the tank a bottle right
under the sheriff's nose and collect for it later. No, this place was not for
Sam Toms. The Hole, folks called it. Two rows of army barracks separated
by a pot-holed dirt road littered with junk and dirty children. And here
in the last unit, with nothing to look out and see but other barracks. No
respect, he thought, and looked at the tossed blankets over the empty
couch where Linda slept. A dog made a neater bed. Mexicans, he thought.

He was a pure man, right from Salvador, a grandson of Rosa, who the
Spanish padres baptized in the tiny adobe on the creek and named the
town after. Santa Rosa. But his offspring . . . Mexicans, Filipinos, whites.
They didn't know the old ways. Hard work. Respect for the old. Nellie
knew. She was an Indian from Rosa, too, even if half of her was Coast
Indian. She knew songs. He felt power when she leaned over him with a
song that led her hand to his heart and pulled him to his feet.

The white doctor said he was going to die. Age, she called it. He
was scared. And no Greta to take care of him. Greta, the German lady
who cooked and cleaned his house and never lifted a quarter out of
his pockets or off his dresser. Good as a wife, he told people. The lady
he hired out of the newspaper after his last wife, who was forty years
younger than him, went back to Guatemala. Good Greta got him up each

morning. She clipped the few whiskers on his chin when they got too long. She ironed his clothes so they were stiff and fresh smelling. She took his arm in the supermarket even though he could walk perfectly fine. Let folks think she was his wife.

"How they do in Germany," she'd say after he complimented her, which was why after Greta got sick and retired, he kept talking about going to Germany even though he had no intention of going. "How they do it in Germany," he'd say.

But his children and grandchildren who came around didn't listen—that is, when they came around at all. They'd bring a pie or pot of chili stew and vie for him. "Come live with me, Gramps. I cook good." "Pops, you'd have your own room in my house." He'd listen and watch for their eyes to roam the house, searching desktops, always coming back to the dresser where he kept his change. More and more he found himself alone, staring at the four walls, opening cans of soup and seeing the clean glow from the sink and kitchen counter fade week by week, month after month.

Orneriness was how he dealt with his family's absence, which drove away whoever still came to see him. "Just rot in your pigsty, old geezer." "Smelly old fool, then don't get out of your chair." Until Linda's mother found him doubled over on his couch one day and hauled him off to the clinic. No, not a stroke. Well, maybe a small one. Just age. The man is nearly a hundred, after all.

She got special foods, took him into her house. Lost among her countless brood and round-the-clock Mexican music, he continued to fade. Try Ensure, the clinic doctor said. Baby food, he said. I'm not dead yet. He wanted someone with songs. He called the cab himself, and it was a steep fare because Nellie was clear across town. And with the cab driver waiting, he carried himself past her flowers, up the steps. And when she sang he knew he'd done the right thing. Something old and true. "Heart sickness," she said in Indian. She opened that place where life was left in him. He could sit up and breathe. She touched and untangled the cramped muscles of his heart. He could feel his pulse. She pulled him to his feet and led him around the room four times before she took him to the front door.

Outside he sucked in the warm morning air as he waited for his cab. Bees hummed around Nellie's flowers, landed, then lifted away, their tiny legs weighted down with pollen. He looked to Grand Avenue beyond

Nellie's yard, saw people here and there. A black woman hollered from her front porch for her children. A man worked under his car, just his legs and heavy work boots showing on the street.

That was when Toms thought of his songs for the first time in ages. People said he looked better. He was livelier.

He had a plan.

He was singing. Before long he couldn't remember whether his plan came from his singing or from his plain thinking. He wasn't going to live in a three-room house with two dozen Mexicans. He'd lost his old place where he had lived with Greta, and Linda's mother held his pension and Social Security. He had to find someone else to take care of him. Some conservator who would let him have his money and some peace. He had to be careful.

He sang in the mornings. He slipped out while the others slept and made his way to a field behind the house. Oak trees were there, and with the early light hitting the curly leaves and green acorns, he remembered his songs one by one. He felt the sun warm his blood, clear his senses. Two things he could still do: sing songs and see right into people.

He set his sights on Ernesto, Linda's older brother. He'd seen the cars come and go, day and night, the visitors Ernesto met in the driveway for no longer than you could blink. You and me, Ernesto, we need our own place. "You're hip, Gramps. Like in, man."

So he got a conservator and a new place. First step.

When the Social Security check came to the new house, Ernesto asked who Sam Toms was. Ernesto matched the name with the papers he signed for the social worker the week before. Gramps. Ernesto cashed the check and turned the money over to Toms. The money was all Toms' now. He paid the rent—his agreement with Ernesto—and had money left. Ernesto shopped for Toms, but that was about all. Too busy coming and going for anything else. Step two: cooking, cleaning, fresh clothes.

He sang his songs in the morning still, on the front porch facing the fairgrounds, before the punks rolled up in their low-slung cars with foam dice hanging from the rearview mirrors. The house was on Temple across from the race track. When Toms sang, only the trainers and their horses were out, going around and around the track. And the sound of birds, and the sun coming over the grandstand in the distance. He sang loudly, then softly, his body lifting and falling with each breath.

He got his answer. It was white, in hard little lumps.

Ernesto could hide nothing. Old man Toms could still see. Like a hawk. And he wasn't going to beg for someone to tidy up the place, or spend an entire afternoon on the phone trying to get someone to wash his clothes. So he kept his eye on two of the greasers, the Big Car one and the No Car one who hung around the park up the street. And each day he went into the plastic bag stuffed inside Ernesto's high-top tennis shoe and pinched a few of the little white lumps. Until the lumps added up.

It happened like clockwork. No Car came over one afternoon when Ernesto was away. Toms was sitting on the front porch. "How much?" he asked No Car and lifted a see-through plastic purse from inside his Pendleton shirt. No Car, who hadn't changed his clothes for a week, fell into the trap. He gave both answers: how much and for what price. Toms unzipped the purse and sprinkled a portion of the cache on his smooth upturned palm. "For washing my clothes," he said. Then he emptied out more of the white magic, in a separate pile. "For keeping your mouth shut."

No Car had the eyes of a child. Too frightened to lie or cheat, which was why he stayed in the park and was No Car. He took the brown paper bags stuffed with dirty laundry and a handful of bills and quarters for the washing machines, and came back with clean clothes for a week and change and got the white stuff Toms wrapped in tinfoil just the way Ernesto did for his customers. "Here," Toms said, slipping No Car another wrapper. "I need a hot meal. Go to the deli. Then come back. I have more for you."

He couldn't pinch from Ernesto forever. He needed Big Car. But Big Car was risky because he wasn't desperate. His eyes were shifty. Toms would have to gamble on the big greaser's greed that he would deliver the goods. "Here you go, old dude," Big Car said, handing Toms the package. "And keep your mouth shut," Toms snapped.

No Car told Toms he'd been cheated out of thirty dollars in the deal, maybe fifty. But it didn't matter to Toms. He figured he would more than get it back. And he did. More than warm meals and clean clothes. Old Toms had girls sitting on his lap. Girls with tattoos like the ones in the old sideshows who took him behind the horses for a dime. White magic got him a peek, now and then even a feel.

If the girls knew Toms' doings, so did others. Ernesto found out and had a fit. "Old sneak, you got my business," Ernesto complained. "We got to go in together." But that wasn't what Toms wanted. Step 3: get Ernesto out of the house.

He had to figure a way around the social worker, a way to get the checks in his name so that he could pay one of the tattooed girls to do things. They'd cook, and clean house better than No Car. He planned to just come out and ask the social worker the next time she came around for her monthly visit. Why not? He was healthy now, not like he was when Ernesto's mother found him. Then, without warning, Ernesto disappeared. As if Toms' wish had been enough to do the trick. Ernesto didn't come back one night, not the next morning either. The cars that finally pulled up around noon were black and white, and the men wore uniforms. They lifted him off the porch, out of his chair, searched him from head to toe, and tore up his neat house.

They didn't handcuff him like they did sixty years before, when they busted his moonshine operation under the hotel on lower Fourth. He was too old. And they gave him a nice room in the jail, where he stayed until the trial. No Car testified that he got the stuff from Toms and Ernesto. He said he'd seen Toms just before the officer found him passed out under a swing set in the park. Toms sat on the hard wooden bench, listening. Occasionally he glanced at the walls and high ceiling of the courtroom. He looked once or twice at No Car but not at the boy's too-frightened-to-lie eyes. Ernesto got prison. Toms was too old. He got sent back to Ernesto's mother with someone from the law to check on him once a month.

But Toms still had steam. He wasn't ready to die, disappear in that crowded house where nobody ever turned off the music. He had clear vision, and Linda walked right into it. Because she was always there, hanging around her mother's house. She was frightened, afraid to be away from people, not just because Pablo, the hood she had been living with, got shot in the head on their front porch awhile back, but because she was basically the kind of person who couldn't be alone. Probably why she went for the hood in the first place. One of the Roseland gang. Toms heard people talk about them. Since she moved back into the house, she yapped incessantly. All about the meaning of life. Why go on living like this, she asked over and over. Her mother was too busy with life to think about things. Toms listened. He told her she needed a fresh start, a new place. They could go in together, and he told her how.

Which is how Toms ended up in the army barracks. In The Hole.

Temporary, he told Linda, because they had to take what was available at the moment. The social worker and the law people thought it was a good idea. The old man and his great-great-granddaughter could take care of one another and keep out of trouble. Linda was on probation, too. Petty larceny.

Linda stuck by Toms, just as Toms had figured. Stuck so close that within two weeks he felt like the spotted mutt with a litter of pups in front of the unit across the way. Sucked dry, day and night. She washed clothes, shopped, cooked, and kept house, even if she wasn't the neatest person in the world. But it was Pablo this and Pablo that. Pablo, whom Toms would have shot if someone hadn't already. And as if Pablo wasn't dead enough, his rivals found where Linda lived and blew out the windows on the back side of the barracks.

"I'm not in the gangs anymore, Gramps," Linda said after she put cardboard over the windows. Which Toms knew was true. She had found new friends and stuck to them like a fly on dung. People from some church and Indians from the Indian Bible study at the YMCA. At first Toms enjoyed the quiet. He could come out of his room where he would retreat from her chatter chatter chatter. But in time she only came around to do her duties, and she was never alone. Toms woke with strangers, ate with them, and closed his bedroom door at night to them. And Linda wanted an extra five dollars for this, ten for that. For the new church. For the missionaries. Toms swore he found money missing. Of course, it would be for a good cause. No way to live, Toms thought.

He hadn't sung his songs since before jail. Oh, maybe those few times at Linda's mother's. But those were feeble attempts. Half way to the field behind the house he hummed in fits and starts. Now he had to sing again. He had to give it all he had. He was failing, and he knew it. He couldn't see his way out.

He sang little by little, more and more each day, while Linda was out with her friends. But he'd get tired, close his eyes, and stop. Some days were better than others, but the better days didn't add up to make a difference. On the eve of his hundredth birthday, he thought of Nellie. She could help him again. It wasn't until the next morning he thought of moving in with her.

The idea came to him straight as the light through the torn cardboard over the window. It stirred and rattled his brain, woke his blood, so he felt as if Nellie already had sung. He had a plan. Why not? She lived alone. He had money. They were both Indians. Old Indians. Toms was surprised he hadn't thought this all out sooner. She was so close, just around the corner. He hadn't felt better in months, years. Today he would be the one to sing. Right in front of Nellie. For her heart. Peace, he thought. Peace. Red roses. Hollyhocks tall as a man. Golden poppies lining the way.

Toms turned from his bowl of Cheerios and squinted at the wall clock above the stove. Seven thirty. Linda would be back by nine. He still wanted to warm up his voice, wake that cricket, but there wasn't enough time, not if he was going to dress himself and pack. Things took time these days. He had to admit that. And he was right. He dabbed himself with a washcloth and splashed Old Spice under his arms and on his neck. Sitting on the bed, he lifted one arm into his shirt, then the other. The same with his pants, slowly one leg, then the other. He labored over every button. When Linda came through the front door, he was tying his shoes.

"Okay, Grandpa, what *are* you doing?" She had seen his dishes on the table and come immediately to his room. "I'm not late. I'm here at the regular time to get you up and fix breakfast."

He straightened, felt a tad dizzy after leaning over his shoes so long. She couldn't even say happy birthday. Did she even know it was his birthday? Did anyone? He was a hundred years old. Toms didn't answer Linda, and she went back to the kitchen. He could hear her doing the dishes.

How could he have thought for a moment about warming up and singing? He still had to pack. At least he dressed himself, and Linda saw that he did. And not to worry about the songs. He had sung on a dime before. And with the way he felt this morning and all that he had done, wasn't luck already on his side? To take care of things now, he only needed Nellie to listen.

He dragged his cardboard suitcase out of the closet and pulled it onto the bed. He packed things for a week, things he would need until he could come back and pack up the rest. A few pairs of underwear, socks, a couple shirts, his everyday brown shoes.

Linda went nuts then. She called her mother. Toms listened.

"Is Mama there? Listen, get Mama. . . . Where is she? As soon as she gets back, tell her that Grandpa's going someplace. . . . No, he won't tell me."

Luck was on Toms' side. But he didn't have all day. He had to work fast. Linda's mother would stop him. Maybe take him back to her house. Why not? She had two times before. He had to get to Nellie and work things out, discuss money and the social worker, before Linda's mother found him. Nellie would have to say she was taking care of him. Lucky he was dressed and finished packing. He buckled the leather strap on his suitcase and made for the phone.

Linda had the phone on her lap. He plopped down on the couch next to her, nearly missing the cushion and hitting the floor. A little too fast, he thought. He caught his breath, then took the phone. Linda gasped and threw her arms up, as if a spider had fallen from the ceiling. The number was easy to remember. 544–TAXI. Toms gave the address and said "Now."

"Grandpa, what is the matter. Talk to me."

Toms started to get up, then settled back on the couch. Conserve energy, he thought. He looked across the room to the bare kitchen table. The room seemed so big, empty. Only then did Toms realize that no one else was there, that he and Linda were alone, seated next to each other. He felt suddenly uncomfortable, as if he should answer her. He wished he was sitting at the table or waiting in his room.

"Pops, haven't you ever had anyone die? Do you know what it's like? I'm doing the best I can."

Toms took hold of his cane, ready to get up. Hah! Have anyone die? He had outlived most of his nineteen children. Didn't she know? Couldn't she see? He was about to tell her, but, thank heavens, the cab driver was at the door.

With slow, careful strokes of her cupped hand, Nellie James brushed the crumbs left from her granddaughter's breakfast off the kitchen table and into the empty wastebasket on the floor. The girl, who sat watching TV in the front room, was in fact Nellie's step granddaughter. She was Nellie's daughter's husband's child from a previous marriage, and anyone might guess as much, or at least wonder, seeing the ten-year-old's golden hair and complexion.

Nellie set the wastebasket under the sink and wiped her hands on the towel folded over the counter. Then she sat down to work on her baskets. She was behind schedule, she had orders to meet, and these days when she baby-sat while her daughter and son-in-law were away, she had precious little time to catch up. She couldn't weave uninterrupted for hours at a time. The girl was well behaved, but like so many single children she depended a great deal on adults for talk and attention. She was all they had to see. Nellie knew because her daughter, Marie, was an only child.

Nellie lifted her large sewing box off the floor and onto the table. Inside the box she found her baskets and the tight rolls of sedge root and redbud bark she kept in neat little rows. She was meticulous. Everything about her: the polished silver tea set on her counter, the way she turned her sleeves up over her wrists, the exact stitching of her coiled baskets. She even surprised herself when she discovered something she overlooked. Mold on the windowsill next to the African violets. A loose stitch.

Her first task was to finish the basket the mayor ordered. It was a small canoe-shaped basket with an exquisite design, if she might say so herself. It was inspired, something she felt had power with the first stitch. Now, as she held the basket in her hands and looped the last stitches of sedge, she hated the thought of giving it up. It occurred to her that she could keep the basket and start another one. Just be late. The mayor wouldn't care. She'd still get paid, and she never dealt with the mayor anyway. It was always his secretary. But then she wouldn't have a basket in the City Hall's display at this year's county fair. And what could possibly silence the acid tongue of her critics faster than this basket in a showcase with her name under it? No traditional Pomo weaver, they said. No art. No inspiration. Just doing it for white-man money. She could hear their hisses, the sharp, drawn out s's when they said she instead of her name.

The trouble started years ago when she married Richard James, for which they would never forgive her. Son of the man who mistreated Indians, none worse than Nellie's own mother, who hung herself in the man's barn after years of abuse. Only Nellie knew the details. They turned their heads when they met Nellie on the road into town. The drunks on lower Fourth shouted things that would shock a sailor. Of course, the son was not the father. But would any of them see that? And now, when the clinic doctor couldn't cure their illnesses, who did they come to with have-mercy-on-me faces? I was wondering, Mrs. James, if maybe you'd

sing just a few of your songs for me? And Nellie sang, helped them, and
got them out her front door before she could think and remember their
turned heads and hateful words. So when Nellie looked up from her
work and saw old man Toms through the screen door, she figured he
wanted the same thing, another dose of what he paid her twenty dollars
for a while back.

"A man's here," her granddaughter had announced.

Nellie saw Toms and tied up the last stitch of her basket. Then she
pulled out the half-finished beaded basket the lady on MacDonald had
ordered. She would get right back to work after Toms left.

She walked through the front room, past the girl watching TV, then
stopped at the door. "You're sick," she said.

Toms said nothing. Then Nellie saw the tall cabdriver coming over
the pebble walkway carrying a cardboard suitcase.

"Is this the place, old man?" the cabdriver asked impatiently and set
the suitcase on the porch next to Toms.

Toms nodded yes and reached into his pocket for change. Realiz-
ing the opportunity to please his client and earn a decent tip, the driver
offered to carry the suitcase inside. The lady on the other side of the
screen door wasn't exactly a spring chicken either, after all. Not nearly as
old as this man, but still nobody to be lugging a big suitcase.

Nellie didn't quite know what happened. Between the time she saw
the suitcase and could think, she found the driver and Toms and the
suitcase in her living room. Toms gave the man four quarters, exact fare,
then looked to Nellie, who stared at the cardboard suitcase on her clean
hardwood floor as if it were a moon rock.

She still hadn't figured things out after Toms was in the kitchen
sitting across from her at the table. She was thinking she would have
to sing for him in there because the girl was on the couch in the front
room. Nellie rarely had the people she sang for into her kitchen. Then
Toms spoke.

"How do you do, Miss James?" he asked. "Pretty little girl you got
out there."

He spoke as if he had just run into her on the street. Formal, she
thought, taking in his pressed black suit for the first time. She felt uneasy,
caught off guard.

"Do you want me to sing?" she asked finally, which was something she never asked. Those who needed her singing asked. She waited for him to answer and twisted a loose strand of sedge between her fingers.

"How many rooms you got here?" he asked.

Then it clicked. The suitcase. The black suit. The fancy talk. She forgot the old man across from her with half his face sagged to his neck and remembered the person Sam Toms. Joker. Moonshine man. Big mouth. Womanizer. And didn't he have songs? Her blood boiled. She felt as if she would burst. She'd known his children. She was their age, probably thirty years younger than him. And here he had come thinking he could move in with her and who knows what else. What was she? An open hotel? A doormat? She wanted to holler, blast him right out of the house. She thought of asking him one more time if he wanted her to sing, just to give him the benefit of the doubt. But she didn't holler or ask the question. She surprised herself. She answered him.

"Two bedrooms," she said.

Toms nodded approval.

"But my granddaughter sleeps in one," Nellie added quickly, gesturing with her chin to the girl in the front room.

Toms raised his eyebrows then followed her chin. "Gee," he said, "I got them in all colors too."

"Oh, yes?" Nellie said. She pushed the loose grey hairs on her forehead under her red bandanna. Just then Toms thought she was beautiful. Something in her gesture. He hadn't really looked at her before. She could be his wife.

"I'm rich," he said.

Nellie folded her hands on the table.

"Real rich," Toms said.

"Oh, yes? How rich?"

"Pension and Social Security. You think that's all? Wrong. Two hundred and thirty-nine bucks for keeping me."

"Hah," Nellie said. "I bet you don't have ten bucks in your pocket."

Toms grinned, showing his white dentures. He was on a roll. He reached into his coat pocket and plopped three twenties, a ten, and some change on the table. Nellie studied the money a moment. Then she gathered it up and dropped it into her canoe basket.

"Well," she said, peering into the basket, "what's this? How do I know I'd get any of it? You got too many grandkids."

"I'll sign it over. Everything. It'll be yours."

"Yes, but what's going to stop those seventeen thousand grandkids of yours from coming around for it?"

"I'll sign them out. Just talk to the social worker. Get papers."

"They'll still come around."

"No. Sign papers for that too. Keep them away."

Nellie considered. "All of them?" she asked.

"Every last one," Toms answered with resolve. "What good are they to me anyway? Just take my money, leave me hanging around."

"Well, that is a shame."

"Yes," said Toms.

"Yeah," Nellie sighed. "You got a point. The young don't think of the old no more."

"That's what I say." She had been testing him, playing around the bait, and now he felt she had taken it hook, line, and sinker. She wasn't only impressed with his money, she understood his situation and felt sorry for him. He watched her turning the basket in her hands.

The blond girl appeared in the doorway. "Grandma, can I go to the store now?"

"Finish your program on TV. Go sit down."

The girl was startled by Nellie's adamant tone. Nellie never talked to her that way. She glanced quickly at Toms, then disappeared.

See, Toms thought. His point exactly. No end to these kids.

Nellie looked at him a long while, then back at the basket of money between her hands. "What else you got?" she asked finally. "What else you got, old Indian man?"

He knew what she meant. Indian. This was it, the last draw. She asked for it. He'd sing his songs loud and clear, so she could hear, and reel her in. He didn't bother to answer her. He cleared his throat, closed his eyes, and to his amazement the songs came loud and clear, just falling from his lips.

He lost track of time. He sang every song he knew. He was proud of his performance, not a cough or even a dry throat when he finished. His tongue and the roof of his mouth felt slippery, smooth. When he opened his eyes, he found Nellie with her head bent, as if in silent prayer, which made him feel good. But then he saw that she was holding her basket toward him, which he didn't understand. She held it up, off the table, and tilted just enough for him to see the money inside.

"Pretty good, heh?" he asked to break the silence. She didn't move. Toms felt something foreboding, frightening. He was looking for words. Then all at once she set the basket down and with both hands slowly pulled it close to her. She lifted her face, and Toms saw immediately what had happened. She'd got away. Her face was tight, flushed purple. But she didn't burst. She uncoiled and struck like a snake.

"Thank you, sir," she hissed. "Now I can lift the spells dirty old men put on good-hearted women. You know, in the right hands these songs can be used as medicine. Antidotes." She was looking down at the basket, turning it in her hands again.

She had caught his songs with her basket. She tricked him, pulled each song out, so that now he was empty. He felt like a drowning man with no sight of land. He grabbed across the table for the basket, but she snatched it up and held it against her breast.

Toms took hold of his cane with trembling hands and bellowed, "Give me back my money!"

"You dirty fool, why should I? You gave it to me, didn't you? Now you're going to take it away from me just like you did from your family?" She looked him straight in the face. "Come on, try it," she dared.

Toms pounded the floor with his cane. "Give me back my money!"

She leaned forward, the basket against her breast, her hard eyes fixed on him with utter contempt. "You fool. Why would I want a man who'd give his money to a strange woman, turn his back on his own family, and then give away songs that might've done good for somebody but of course never did because the man is low-down rotten to the core."

"Give me back my money!" Toms ranted. He felt himself sinking now beneath the force of her wrath. In desperation he lifted his cane and took a swipe across the table at Nellie. She jumped back in her seat, and the cane swept over the table, knocking her sedge roots and half-finished beaded basket to the floor. "Son of a bitch," Toms cursed. "God-damned white man whore. . . . White lover . . ." He went to swing his cane again but couldn't. His heart tightened, his innards turned this way and that. He was out of breath. The fight was over.

His words echoed in Nellie's ears. She wasn't moving now either. She was still leaning back in her seat, the basket clutched tight to her body, as if waiting for Toms' next strike. But her face was pale, expressionless. In a split second she saw her life in countless scenes and situations from those days and times on lower Fourth to this very morning. Toms had hit her square in the heart with that which never left her, that which she packed on her back the way a stinky old possum packs its stinkier young. Spiteful pride. She was stunned. She was mean and she knew better.

"Grandma, what happened?" The girl was in the doorway.

"Watch TV," Nellie said, letting out a long breath. She set her canoe basket down.

Toms took hold of his cane and managed to get to his feet. Instinctively, he turned and made for the door. He moved like a windup doll, slow, deliberate, in one direction.

Nellie sat looking at Toms' money in her basket. She heard the screen door open and close. She thought of her granddaughter and found her watching TV. She poked at the loose strands of her hair, straightened her bandanna, and got up. She called a cab, and then went outside with the basket.

She found Toms standing at the bottom of her steps in a daze, glassy-eyed. She took his arm and helped him to sit down. She set his cane against his legs, where he could reach it. Then she put the basket in his hands and situated it so it rested in his lap. She stood a minute, before going, to make sure the basket didn't tip or fall and spill out the money.

She had forgotten about the suitcase. Inside, she found it still like a moon rock in the middle of her living room. She dragged it across the floor and out onto the porch. Then she went back in and watched through the screen door until the cab left with Toms.

She thought she'd get back to weaving, pick up where she left off. Then, in the kitchen, she saw her beaded basket and roots on the floor. She had forgotten about the mess. Among the loose strips of sedge and redbud bark she saw the crumbs from breakfast that had missed the wastebasket.

"Grandma," the girl said, coming up behind Nellie, "I'm glad that old man left."

No great accomplishment, Nellie thought to herself.

"Grandma, now can I please go to the store?"

Nellie didn't answer her.

"Grandma, I need a dollar for the store."

Nellie turned, half-facing her granddaughter. "Look in my purse," she said.

Toms didn't remember the cab driver steering him into the couch. The driver, who took the dollar bill out of the canoe basket for the one-dollar fare, offered to call an ambulance or a doctor, whatever Toms wanted. But Toms didn't hear him. At six in the evening, just before Linda came home, Toms was still sitting on the couch, not sure how long he had been sitting, or even if he had gone anywhere at all. He saw the crumpled blankets next to him lit by the dull light from the front window and thought Linda was still sitting there. She was asking him about having people die, and he was trying to answer her.

» The Progress of This Disease

The doctor takes me alone into her office, as if Jeanne, my daughter, doesn't know the truth already, as if leaving her alone in the waiting room won't tell her the kind of news I'm getting about her. I've been through this before. I know all the rooms on this end of the clinic, both of the beige examination rooms with their striped curtains and oil paintings of plump-faced Indian children. Doctor Kriesel's office is the same. Only behind her on the wall there is a different kind of painting. Against a black background a hand holds a spread of eagle feathers.

"That represents healing," the doctor says, finding me gazing at the picture. "Sit down, Anna." I sit, glance at her, then back at the picture, then back at her.

"Betty at the front desk said it's a medicine man. Gives me strength as a doctor. You know, in this clinic."

I want to tell her I'm no Indian from the bush, that I'm a Christian and don't believe in any of that old stuff. Truth is, I don't want to tell her what I'm thinking, because I don't want to think any more than I want to hear what she is going to tell me.

"You do like it, don't you?"

"Oh, yes," I answer. She forgets that we have talked about this before, about what the painting means and whether or not I like it. The conversation always goes the same way. She is confident, knows all about the painting. Then, remembering the kind of news she must tell me, she wilts, slumps in her white coat, listless as a sick gull. Her round blue eyes are like a child's and search the room, maybe for a picture or something that might tell her what to say. I tell her I know Jeanne is sick, and then she straightens and talks about red blood cells and white blood cells. But today she surprises me. Something else happens. She doesn't wilt, says nothing about cells. She hands me an x-ray across her mahogany desk, and before I have a chance to study it, before she explains anything, she asks if I understand the progress of this disease.

"Yes," I answer.

It is still early when Jeanne and I walk back to the parking lot outside the clinic. The sun hovers above the hills, hits the clinic roof and the tops of trees in the lot. Jeanne skips a few steps just before the car, then turns and announces, "We're going to the ocean today. Right now, Mom." Her resolute voice is at odds with her lighthearted skipping a moment ago. You'd think just another sign that at fourteen she is still flip-flopping her way into adulthood. Like the way she experiments with makeup and then spends hours arranging and rearranging her dolls. But she is sick, and she knows it. The pain in her back last week, the three doctor visits, the now-and-then loss of feeling in her legs. I must be careful with her today, I keep telling myself. Follow routine, which is about all I can do, given what just happened in the doctor's office, what I saw. Stick to routine. For Jeanne.

"We're Indians of the road," she says as I pull the one-eyed Ford out of the lot.

"Onto the road," I say. She stares ahead with eyes in her thin face like oversized marbles. Her skin looks yellowish, her lips too dark, the color of blackberry stains on a person's fingers. I say nothing. She is determined, almost fierce. Like me, she's stubborn, insistent. We know our limits, we have our ways of doing things, like the trips we take after the clinic.

I pinch from what little I have for these trips. Me and Jeanne eat at restaurants I can't afford. I leave my seven other children all day. We go east to Sonoma, where Jeanne likes to have lunch in the park and watch the ducks and geese. Lots of times we go to the coast and sit on the beach. When she was stronger, we picked seaweed for Grandma and Uncle, my mother and her brother. I always tell stories, fill the road with talk, mostly about things I remember from my youth, when Mama and I moved from place to place after we left the reservation. So much has changed. In some places endless rows of new houses cover the land. But I see the signs, an old gatepost that a contractor missed, an apple tree left from an orchard, and I am amazed at how quickly I remember things.

Today I take 116 west, and where the two-lane highway opens onto the scrub oak dotted hills, I tell about the dairyman's wife. She was so fat she couldn't get out of bed. Mama worked all morning just to get her to sit up so she could push her into the special chair the dairyman had built. Still, the lady often missed the chair, or half-missed it, so that she dripped in fleshy gobs to the floor. Then Mama's work was really cut out for her. She had to get the woman up.

"She ate too much butter," Jeanne says. "Now tell about the sheep farmer."

I nod, and as I start about the farmer and his errant sheep, I see the late spring sweetpeas, pink and white along the road, and the clumps of bright yellow scotchbroom on the hills like billowy clouds, soft as feather pillows.

I talk until the ocean and then go north to Bodega Bay. Jeanne wants to eat at The Tides, where we can watch the fishing boats. I tell her it's too early, that the place isn't open yet. She says we can wait. The ocean is flat, clear as glass. We're quiet until we get to the pier, where I park in the empty lot and me and Jeanne find a bench by the water.

We watch a large fishing boat berth at the dock below us, curly haired men in overalls coming onto the deck from nowhere and jumping to the dock, working quickly, frantically with ropes to secure the vessel. The men disappear for a time, the boat looks empty. Then slowly two or three come back and jump onto the boat, then two or three more. A short, heavy man in a blood-smeared apron pushes a wooden cart nearly as high as he is to the boat. Then we see the fish, piles of silver salmon in a cage being lifted by an automatic crane from somewhere in the boat's bowels. The huge cage drips water, and the fish jump and writhe, their metallic silver bodies catching the sun. I tell Jeanne how we used to come here and get big salmon for five cents a pound and how Grandma remembered when us Indians had them for free.

"White people," Jeanne snarls, imitating Mama in a bad mood.

"Remember your Bible," I say. "All people are equal. Some of us just behave better."

She is suddenly sleepy, I can see it in her face, and she does not respond to me. Usually I get a "humph" or "tsst" when I mention the Bible. Like any kid, I suppose. The morning sun is warm, bright in her face now. Santa Rosa will be a scorcher today. I hope that Mama will take the kids to the Swim Center. She got her Social Security this week.

"Gee," I say, "Mama and me used to come here all the time. Hitch a ride with the dairyman when we didn't have a car."

"Mom," Jeanne says, as if far away, already half asleep. "You and Grandma were real Indians of the road. You went everywhere. We never moved, just stayed in the same house in Santa Rosa. We never went anywhere."

"We are now," I say, but I'm talking to myself. Her eyes are closed, her head tilted against the back of the bench. I put my arm around her, under her head, and wait, watching the men below me tossing the fish, one at a time, into the wooden cart on shore.

I'm not surprised, given the doctor's office and all, that I should find myself on this pier. Funny how things turn out. I can picture Mama standing not far from where that wooden crate sits, her hair and tattered calico dress flapping in the cold wind.

"I'll clean fish," she hollered. "Clean fish," she repeated as if old man Jones couldn't hear.

Jones's boat rocked up and down in the rough water, straining at the ties, and he stood on the deck before a stack of empty crab nets and looked at Mama as if he couldn't see any better than he could hear. He was half white. He had fine features, but the sun and his shabby white beard made him look even darker than Mama.

"Clean fish," she yelled at the top of her lungs. "Any amount."

He squinted. Mama called again, even louder. She waited. At last he seemed to recognize her, but he said nothing. He planted his feet, and his eyes shot back, crazy, pointed like a mad bull's. He took a deep breath and boomed. "Cursed," he roared. "Cursed."

Mama's calico blew in the wind. She stood, unflinching. He told her to leave. "Bad luck," he shouted.

"You're no Christian," Mama burst out. "You're no high-brow like they say. You're a God-damned, low, stinking Indian worse than your white-man whore mother . . ." Mama hollered on, her face colored with rage. But it was no use. The wind pushed her hateful words back into her throat. Jones, with his arms crossed over his chest, wasn't touched. Mama wouldn't get the job.

I hadn't realized how sore and tired I was until I picked up my cardboard suitcase again. We'd already come ten miles, not on any road but mostly through the bush, picking our way along fences and black woods. Mama hoisted the gunnysack that held everything we owned over her shoulder and started off the pier. She stopped once and looked back at Jones. She spit and laughed. We followed the coast highway south. Luckily we didn't walk far. We came to a bridge, and like a wounded animal Mama dropped under it.

A shallow creek ran below the bridge. Mama knelt as if she was going to wash her face, but then she slumped back against the gunnysack and fell asleep. I put my head on the suitcase and tried to do the same, but the cars and lumber trucks going over the bridge kept me awake. Mama slept like a log.

It had been all I could do the night before to keep up with Mama and lug my suitcase, and now I couldn't sleep. The world sat still, but my mind raced on. I looked to Mama and saw clumps of watercress with tiny white flowers by her feet. I couldn't ask her what had happened, given her mood, even if she was awake. She was temperamental, and you knew to stay out of harm's way when she was irritable. I knew Auntie Sipie had died, but I couldn't figure out what else had happened. I was nine or ten, and my mind couldn't take in an adult's amount of knowing. I needed Uncle, Mama's brother who lived with us and took care of me. He cooked, even washed my clothes, when Mama worked or took off with a man friend. When she came back, grumpy and empty-handed, I kept under him like I would an umbrella in a storm. He'd answer my questions. Once, after some kids teased me, I asked him who my father was. "Your mother doesn't know," he said plain as day. Then he took the gold watch that always dangled from his coat pocket and, rubbing it between his thumb and forefinger, he whispered, "so you're magic, daughter of every flower that grows." He said this was my secret, that it was like the doctoring songs he sang when I had a cold or stomachache.

Somehow, in the events of the last day, Uncle got lost. He wasn't

home when Auntie Sipie's man came with the news. When Mama went
down to Sipie's house, which was just a few doors away on that tiny ten-
house reservation, he didn't come in. And still later, when Mama came
back acting crazy, like a chicken with a coyote in the yard, he still didn't
come. Mama bolted the door and pulled the shades. Later, Sipie's man
came back and asked for Uncle, and Mama went outside. The next thing
I knew we were packing, and when Mama finally grabbed my arm and
yanked me out the front door, away from the sleeping reservation, we
were alone.

It must've been almost noon by the time Mama woke. She lifted herself up and stretched. She looked around, and when she spotted me, she
seemed surprised. She leaned over the creek, cupped her hands in the
water and patted her face.

"We're moving," she said resolutely. "I know what we're going to
do." She seemed lighter, refreshed. She straightened her hair and brushed
the sand off her dress.

"Now, come on, get up," she said and turned, starting up the bank to
the highway. She swung the gunnysack over her shoulder.

"What about Uncle?" I said.

She stopped. I'd come up behind her on the slope. She turned, and
the only thing I could think of was a giant, a bear. I couldn't move, and
her face got darker and darker. "Don't you . . ." she snarled. "Don't you
ever mention him again. Don't you let me or any Indian ever hear that
name. It's all his fault. His foolery. He caused your Auntie Sipie to die."
She leaned her fierce face into mine. "I'll leave you in the woods, you
hear? I'll leave you with the white people."

I didn't look away. I needed her to forgive me.

Mama's a big woman, wide but also tall, which is unusual for a Pomo.
It's what the dairyman must've noticed when he found us trudging south
on the highway. We'd hardly been up from the bridge ten minutes when
he pulled his truck off the road. He was a burly man with a head of black
curls and a face the red color of a cooked crab. He asked Mama to lift one
of the heavy milk cans off the back of his truck. He said he'd pay her. She
set her sack on the road and without saying a word lifted a shiny can and
set it on the ground. She lifted another, then another, until she had half a
dozen cans down. The man watched and then told her to put them back.

"You want a job, don't you?" he asked Mama when she finished. He was looking at me and Mama's gunnysack.

She never said yes or no, but the next thing I knew we were riding in the back of the truck, bouncing around against the milk cans. Mama couldn't have known where we were going, she couldn't have known about her job, about the dairyman's wife, who she would care for and lift in and out of bed. But bracing herself against the cans, she looked peaceful, her head lifted triumphantly as she watched the road disappear after each turn.

The dairyman put us in a one-room shack next to the milk barn. It had a woodburning stove that heated the place good, and that's about all it had. Turned out the dairyman and his wife were Portuguese, like half the other dairy farmers in the county, and from that first afternoon until the day we left, we ate Portuguese food—stews, soups, and sweet bread. We ate in the front room, where the lady—Marie was her name—slept and took her meals. The kitchen table was there and the radio. Mama and Marie became more than friends, they became inseparable, which was odd, given Mama's dislike for white people. Marie smelled sour, just the way Mama described white people, and she felt sorry for herself, which was something else Mama didn't like. She'd cry about how she was fat and sick, rubbing her tiny round hands into her massive face. Still, Mama would sit with her all afternoon, talking and looking out the window to the fields of black and white cows on either side of the rutted road that led up to the house. At night the two of them played cards until the wee hours of the morning. The dairyman became a stranger in the house, if he hadn't always been. He came into the front room as if he was asking permission to do so. It was no surprise when he moved our pallet beds into the house.

Mama changed. There were no men in her life and no drinking, none of her moody hangovers. She didn't talk about people, gossip, the way she used to. When we'd see Indians in town, she'd look the other way. She pulled her once-loose hair back in a tight bun, and even though she got her dresses from Saint Vincent de Paul, she wore them like new, clean and pressed stiff. But there was more. She doted on me. She watched to make sure I ate all my meals. Each morning before school I stood at attention as she straightened my dress, evened my shoelaces, added a ribbon to my hair. She walked me to the bus stop, and she'd be there waiting every afternoon. She went over my lessons with me. If she didn't understand something, she'd ask Marie, my other mother. At night she stayed with me until I fell asleep. She sat straight and hard, her body shaped into a perfect rectangle by the corset she cinched herself into each day.

Mama and Marie argued sometimes about things like what time to eat or how much salt to put in a stew. Mama had an obsession about beating Marie at cards, and once after Marie won five nights straight, Mama asked me to stay up and watch to see if Marie cheated. I watched the longest time, then I fell asleep. When I awoke, sometime in the early morning, there they were with the light still on over Marie's bed. Two big women, the light one sprawled back in the bed, the dark one slumped in a chair, and a stack of cards scattered between them on the crumpled white sheets.

For all Mama's hard work, Marie still got sicker and sicker. Marie wasn't well to begin with, after all. But Mama wouldn't see it. She fought Marie's failing health with the same mad determination she had for everything else she did in those days. When Marie couldn't sit up by herself, Mama pulled her forward in the bed and then let go of her, leaving her to sit by herself for as long as she could. Mama counted the seconds on her wristwatch until Marie collapsed on her pillows. Toward the end, Mama got so crazy with this it seemed she was torturing Marie, whose lifeless arms and head flopped this way and that each time Mama pulled her up. And when the moment came and Mama couldn't coax another breath out of Marie, Mama sighed and looked as if she'd just lost a hand of cards, her eyes searching the bed, the still body, for a sign she'd been cheated. She pulled the shades over the window, looked back once at Marie propped up in her bed and staring blankly, then left the house forever.

We didn't have to move. The dairyman never told us to go. He knew after Mama asked him to move our pallet beds back to the one-room shack that we wouldn't stay. It turned out that he helped us move. He got us a job with the sheep farmer five miles down the road. After the dairy ranch, we just went from place to place. The sheep farm, another dairy, the orchards. Mama's size and determination made her the best at whatever she did, whether digging post holes for the sheep farmer or milking cows. And she always kept herself clean, in a dress with her hair pulled back in a shiny bun. Somewhere along the way, she picked up the Bible and spent all her evenings and spare hours reading furiously. She would be the one who decided when we needed to move on. Certain things set her off: twin calves drowned in a well, the sheepherder's cousin who carried a talking parrot on his shoulder. "I can't tell them that bird's scaring the sheep off," she said. "They won't listen. They can't see the truth." She quoted the Bible. She had answers for everything.

I came to detest her doting care. She was plain overbearing. Of course, now I was sixteen, the age to revolt, and a boy named Joaquin Copaz gave me good reason. It was on an apple ranch, where we lived in a nice cottage next to the rancher and where Mama was the field foreman, which are the two reasons the Indian workers didn't give Mama mind to leave right away—she didn't have to live in the tent camp with them, and she didn't have to talk with them about anything beyond business. Some were our own relatives from the reservation—Mama's first cousin Zelda and her daughters, Pauline, Rita and Billyrene, girls my age. I was happy to see them, make friends, never mind Mama's proclamations that they were heathens and dirty. It had been six years or more since I had talked to other Indians.

Joaquin was the kind of boy a girl notices, a boy whose mouth moves just so when he talks, whose black eyes settle in yours like nothing before, who makes you senseless. I was a late bloomer, sixteen, like I said. I knew he liked me. He'd hide behind the apple trees along the road, waiting for me to get off the school bus. And later, down by the creek, where I'd hide from Mama and visit my cousins, he'd sit with the other boys and watch me. What I didn't know was that half the other girls liked him too.

After school I changed out of my new skirts and blouses into dungarees and sleeveless work shirts. I wanted to look like the other Indians, who didn't go to school. I knew Mama was suspicious, given my absence from the house after school, and I should have figured she'd follow me one day. When she did, she found me with the others, and for the first time I was sitting in the grass next to Joaquin. She stood above the creek, a dark, imposing figure casting judgment on all of us. I was the only one who had to answer to her.

That night it was warfare. The quiet, smoldering kind. Mama's specialty, what happened before her spewing proclamations, so you never quite knew when she would erupt. I'd seen it when she was mad at a boss. I watched her explode alone in the house. Now it was me, her and me. Finally, at the dinner table, it started, but was over as quickly as it began.

"That boy's your third cousin," she said, matter of fact.

I was surprised by her tone, expecting something worse. "We're tangled up with everybody," I retorted.

She looked at me for the longest time. "That's right," she said. Then her voice cracked and she whispered, "so don't get any ideas."

She excused herself, actually said "Excuse me," and left the table. I didn't think then, but of course she was a hundred feet underwater in her own loneliness.

I cared only what the others thought, my friends and Joaquin. None of the Indians liked Mama. They said she was stuck-up, white-acting. Rumor had it she had married the dairyman, since people saw her in town with him and had no idea about his sick wife at home. So I used Mama's finding me with Joaquin to tell the others—who I went right back to the next day—all the things I found wrong with her. The rock-hard corset, her Bible preaching, her friendliness with the white bosses, which wasn't quite true but which would certainly stir up my friends. But something was wrong. At first I thought maybe they pulled back from me because I was disrespectful of my mother. Then I worried they thought I was too much like her, white-acting with my going to school and all. They wouldn't talk to me, just listen, their shared silence signaling their collusion.

Joaquin brought me flowers every day. We held hands, and once, above the creek bank away from the girls, he kissed me. I was embarrassed when a couple of his friends jumped out from behind the brush, hooting and hollering. So was he, since he was the rare kind of Indian boy who didn't make hate and insecurity his best friends. He didn't need to show off. He was a gem. Believe me, if things had been different, Mama would've blessed us both, had us married in a heartbeat. But that would never happen, Mama or no Mama. Billyrene, my older cousin with the mouth, fixed things just the way the girls wanted.

It was at our hangout place by the creek.

"Your mother's no Bible lady," Billyrene cracked, breaking the silence.

I didn't really understand her, what she meant.

"She's cursed. A witch, just like her brother who killed our aunt."

Joaquin sat up straight, resting a bouquet of snapdragons on his knee.

"Oh, don't try to defend her, Joaquin," Billyrene said. "I can't believe you don't know. You're probably already cursed just by kissing her. . . . Tell him, Anna, tell him what your uncle did. . . ."

I watched the other girls shift in the grass. They looked with confident amusement back and forth at Joaquin and me.

"Go on, tell him how your uncle cursed some lady so she died, and then it backfired on Sipie. . . . Tell him how the lady died all covered with grey snot and afterbirth. Yes, and how we found Auntie the same way. Tell him how you're cursed. The only reason you and your mother live is because you're evil too. Tell him. . . ."

Billyrene's voice echoed. I saw the snapdragons strewn on the ground next to me. I didn't look back at Joaquin, but before I left I saw all I needed to—the girls' jealous faces emboldened and relieved by Billyrene's spiteful victory.

Of course, I knew we'd move after I told Mama, but I wasn't thinking that far ahead when I finally burst out with everything at the dinner table that night. I just talked on, let go with everything, but my voice was small and broken with all I knew for the first time.

Cancer was the word Billyrene told Jeanne. Billyrene with the mouth. Billyrene who moved up the street to haunt me with her forked-tongue kindness. Oh, Anna, is there anything I can do for you? Watch the kids while you're at the doctor's? It must not be easy with Albert in the bars again. So glad you and me are neighbors now, Anna. Go ahead, I think, rub it in, Billyrene. No one invited you with your how many kids from how many men to this place. The United Nations flag should fly over your front porch. Turned out just like your mother, who'd passed out drunk so the men could carry her on a stretcher from room to room. But I don't speak. At least I can stop my tongue, and I'm ashamed that what I shouldn't be thinking comes up so fast.

At first we used the word *ache*. It started that way, just below the abdomen. That and tiredness. Then chemotherapy and no more ache. But eight months later, ribs and hipbones showed under skin that was not the right color, and ache was back and everywhere. Then it was *sick*. When Jeanne came through the front door with the word *cancer*, I surprised

myself. I sat down with her calm as day. "Yes," I said. I was relieved, and
as I talked in a way Jeanne could understand, the word actually felt good,
like a ball of dough that I could shape in my hands. The only time Jeanne
asked if she would get better was right then. "Yes," I said.

I took myself to the library, read books, learned so much about the
disease that I came to speak its language, which is a hollow tongue of
numbers and strange words. That's why Doctor Kriesel goes on with me
about counts and cells. But I moved beyond her. I read about Laetrile,
coffee enemas, diets of brown rice and sprouts, support groups—none of
which I had time or money for. Visualization seemed the ticket. It's free
for the effort. Picture the body healthy. See flowers and things. Green is a
good color.

So at first Jeanne and I took rides to find open pastures where we
parked the car and sat, letting the color green fill our eyes and enter our
bodies. Jeanne saw cows and got bored. Then, to keep her happy and
fill the road as I drove frantically looking for an empty spread of green,
I started telling stories. I told about me and Mama and all the different
people we knew, and Jeanne seemed to like the stories. Now all I do is
call up the same stories again and again while we drive here and there for
lunch or whatever. To tell the truth, Jeanne's not crazy about the stories. I
know. It's the ride that pleases her. It's the break from home, where mo-
notony leaves the door wide open to pain and fear. "Grand Avenue," she
complains as we turn onto our street.

When we first moved to our place I had marveled at all the room.
Three bedrooms, such a big house. And the name of the street had a
ring—Grand Avenue. Even if it was at the south end of Santa Rosa, where
the poor and what-have-you's lived. I'd walk out in the evenings with
my two kids in my hands and look at that street sign like it was magic.
Here I was a free woman living in the city, a woman like any other with
two kids and a husband. No more running from pillar to post so Mama
could help half the countryside live and die. I put the rent down, first and
last month's, and Mama came to live with me. Stores. A shopping center.
Parks with goldfish ponds. No one we knew.

Reality is like the sun on a summer morning. It burns right through
the fog. As I always think in looking back, Vietnam got Joaquin Copaz,
and Albert Silva got me. Two kids became eight and a husband's earnings
became a welfare check. I peel apples at the cannery when there's work,

and Mama's burdened in caring for my kids. Half the Indians in town live up the street or around the corner, and of those, too many are on the front porch asking for Uncle.

We found Uncle preaching on a street corner uptown. He wasn't poor, though he lived in a room above the Sixth Street mission. And he wasn't crazy. He'd organized a Bible study group for Indians at the YMCA and took orders directly from the local minister. Mama and I were stopped at a light when we spotted him. "Pull over," she said, and before I stopped the car she was out and making her way across the street. When I caught up, he was reading from his Bible. He was so much smaller than I remembered, shorter than Mama. He wore the same Stetson hat and dark suit, but his clothes fit him loosely, and there was no gold watch chain dangling from his coat pocket. Mama answered him, naming the chapter and verse he read. This went on for half an hour, him reading and stopping long enough only for her to identify the passage. What I didn't see as I stood there waiting was all that was understood between them.

They never inquired about one another's lives. They never said goodbye. Uncle closed his Bible, and Mama and I went back to the car.

We were on our way to the unemployment office. I'd managed to get enough time at the cannery to stand in line there. We drove in silence. Mama didn't say anything about what had just happened with Uncle until I was parked. She waited until I stopped the motor.

"What happened was in the past," she proclaimed. "The rest is the devil's black heart, feeding itself on those uncertain souls who know no better." Her voice was so plain and even you'd have thought she was reading. She skipped a beat, then added, "Uncle's always lived with us. His Social Security will help us out now."

She made herself clear: whatever Uncle did or didn't do didn't matter, and he was coming to live with us. That much the two of them understood.

It happened like clockwork the next day. Uncle shows up in his dark suit and Stetson hat with a shopping bag full of his belongings in each arm. That was eight o'clock in the morning. By noon he was washing the kid's clothes with Mama. He was a regular fixture in our house. Even the kids didn't notice him anymore.

Mama and Uncle turned out to be two peas in a pod. They found in each other what they had missed for years: company. They did everything

together. Shop, cook, clean house, disappear each night for their Bible
meeting at the YMCA. For the first time I saw how they were brother and
sister. Their broad, dark features, that slant in their eyes, the fat hands and
short fingers. But more than that, more than anything else, it was something about their posture that drew my attention to them as two people.
Something I'd seen in Mama the last few years but never really thought
of, and something I would see in Zelda, Billyrene's mother, and the rest
who'd come to the front porch for Uncle. They were slightly stooped,
bent in a way each and every one of them understood. It was what Mama
and Uncle showed each other straight away on the street corner that day.

It bothered me.

There was something secret between them. When they peered up
at you from their lowered faces, they seemed to be telling you that they
knew something you didn't know. At first I thought a lot about the un-
speakable: Uncle and what happened to Auntie Sipie. Mama only alluded
to the matter, saying it was in the past, which was the first and last time
she had talked about it since that day many years ago when we were
under the bridge. I'd heard about it, though, and not just in front of
Joaquin. At the dance hall when I was around the other Indian girls, I'd
catch the words "her uncle" and see the furtive glances full of suspicion
and curiosity. I ignored them. The devil's black heart feeding itself, as
Mama would say. But there was nothing furtive or suspicious about the
eyes of Mama or Uncle or any of those folks who came for Uncle. Nothing that spelled out whatever had happened in the past but something
that was bigger, bolder. Something you see in the eyes of religious zealots
bent on converting you. A secret you could know for the asking that
would change your miserable life.

But there was nothing for me to ask. I read the Bible. I struggled the
best I could.

More and more people came for Uncle, which brought me added
aggravation. Billyrene, for instance. Zelda's on friendly terms with the
family, and Billyrene, who Zelda stays with now and then, learns all about
us. A perfect setup for Billyrene to come in each night after her mother
leaves with Uncle and revel in my hard luck. This wasn't the first I'd seen
of Billyrene since she snuffed my romance with Joaquin. She'd be at the
dance hall around the time I was dating Albert. She was somewhat pitiful
since she was so overweight and plain. She was the last girl the boys asked

to dance, the first to have their babies. She asked me once *what* Albert was. "Portuguese," I answered proudly.

She's never mentioned the Joaquin incident, and she'd be embarrassed if I did. True, she's nosey and jealous, but I suppose she's not so unusual. I've found lots of women like her. It just seemed like she was always sitting in my house, all two hundred and fifty pounds of her, absorbing every detail of my life and reminding me of it. Like I said, I wasn't mad after Jeanne carried the word *cancer* from her to me. It was just her, and I had an excuse to strike back. "Billyrene, you've got diarrhea of the mouth and nothing in your brain to stop it. You've always been like that," I told her. And I could've said a lot more, but there was no satisfaction in it. She hung her head, the way she did when she was standing against the wall at the dance hall, and like the sorrowful and spiteful fool she was then, coming back each Saturday night, she'd keep coming back to me.

I try to be charitable. I make a point of it. I take what's good in the Bible and use it in my life. Like I said, I can stop my tongue from spilling what's in my head. But things got to me when Jeanne got sick and then sicker. My snapping at Billyrene was just the first sign. I got so bad Billyrene left one day without me having to ask her. Albert had an excuse to stay out and drink all night. I got to be like a porcupine using its stiff quills to keep the world at a safe distance. I couldn't stand it: everybody knew my business, they never stopped asking about Jeanne. A hundred pairs of eyes were on me, offering prayers, condolences, and secrets I didn't want to know existed.

Uncle's not the jolly man I remember. He is quiet, solemn. Neither he nor Mama push their ideas at you with their tongues. Neither one asked if they could pray over Jeanne. I asked.

One night while I was punching down frydough as if I was killing a wild dog, Mama took my arm. She surprised me since she is not the kind of person to touch you out of the blue. It was early, before dinner, and she took me out the back door. We sat on the porch step overlooking a backyard of junked car parts and untamable weeds and blackberry vines.

"It's a mess," she said, and I didn't know if she was referring to the yard or Jeanne's situation or both.

She was gazing at the yard. Then she turned and took my arm again. "Honey," she said, as if I was ten, "you can't let this bother you so. You got to relax, let go." I still wasn't sure what she meant by this. But it didn't

matter. Her voice was like cool water on a burn. I'd pushed and pulled
the world too long. Made lunches. Made doctor appointments. I needed
a mother. I looked at her soft brown hand on my parched, dough-dusted
skin and fell into her uncontrollably. "Pray for me," I cried. "Pray for
Jeanne."

It was a weak moment, as I would find out. My stubborn self with all
its insights would rise. That same night Uncle and the congregation didn't
go to the YMCA. They settled in the front room, about a dozen of them.
Jeanne lay on the sofa, her tired face propped up by a pillow. The lights
went off and the crowd of hunched men and women gathered over her.
I didn't like the darkness and the flickering candles that Zelda and Mama
held. Hocus-pocus. Staging, and a lot of trickery, so the secret in the eyes
and bent backs might reveal itself. This was how my mind was going.

"Our Holy Father, forgive us our sins," Uncle started as he stood between Zelda and Mama with his open Bible. "Forgive us," he continued
with his voice rising. "Forgive us who knew no better. Forgive us the
pain in our lives." He kept on about forgiveness, which angered me. Then
in my anger, in my reason for being upset, I saw their secret. They accepted their sins, admitted guilt. Zelda her numerous nameless affairs.
Mama her lonesome pride. Uncle the deaths of two women. I picked the
secret up in Uncle's first words. They were praying for themselves.

Eventually, Uncle turned to Jeanne. He invoked the Holy Ghost.
He was earnest, faithful. He put everything in God's hands. It was God's
will whether Jeanne got better or worse. He prayed in a way that he
couldn't lose.

Jeanne and I are the first ones in the restaurant. We sit at a table with
a view of the fishing boat, now emptied of fish. She has taken two bites of
her tuna sandwich, maybe a couple spoonfuls of her chowder. She looks
out the window and she is very pale. Already one trip to the bathroom.
She can't hold anything down.

"How long did it take them to empty the boat?" she asks, turning her
head on her stick shoulders. She is trying to make conversation with me,
follow routine. But her voice is thin, strained, like fine lace stretched to
its limit.

I help her. "About half an hour," I say, and look at the vessel secured
tightly to the dock.

She looks at her food, then out the window, then at me.

"Mom," she says, "Rachel has been nice to me."

Rachel is Billyrene's daughter, about a year or two older than Jeanne. She's like her mother, petty and jealous. Why shouldn't she be nice to you, I want to say and follow routine. But that's not what Jeanne wants now. Her voice is broken, torn. She has given up on our routine. This is it. I must talk.

"Mom," she says. "Mom, everyone's nice to me now." She keeps her eyes on me.

"Yes," I say.

"Mom, they know I'm gonna die, huh?"

"Well . . ." I stutter. "People should be nice no matter what." She looks back at her food then out to the blue, blue water beyond the fishing boat. She knows. She knows I know. We know. There, as much as I can say. There, it's out. Acceptance. What I should've seen two weeks ago when Uncle and his congregation prayed. My sin: my blinding drive against hard luck, against the curse. It was like a train coming all along. You watch it, hear the whistle blow, the rumbling of the tracks as it draws nearer and nearer. But then it's something else, something that hits you in the back while you're watching that train. Jeanne knew I'd been hit. Our routine, our drive today, wasn't working. I tried. We both tried. But I'd been hit. She just couldn't see how. Couldn't see Doctor Kriesel hand me that x-ray. Couldn't see my face, feel my insides burst, as I glanced at the picture and saw not the dark masses in a sea of lighter grey, not the tumors, but the pieces of snot and afterbirth that covered Auntie Sipie, the story that wouldn't die.

"Yes," I repeated to Dr. Kriesel, letting out all that I held within me. "Yes, I understand."

I wrapped Jeanne's sandwich. The soup I couldn't take. I hate wasting. As we drive silently into Santa Rosa, I wonder what will change, if anything. I'm thinking about little things that have been a part of our lives. Jeanne's skipping after the doctor visits. Her complaint "Grand Avenue" as we turn onto our street. My endless stories. I think to tell her that our ancestors are from this place, from a village along Santa Rosa Creek. That was so long ago, way before Mama's time, before the tribe got split up and the handful of survivors went west to the coast or north to the reservations. But what's the point of mentioning it? Because it's something I haven't told her, I tell myself. Something she should know. . . . Then, in my mind, I hear what she would say: So we all came back.

She's slumped in her seat, drowsing, her head showing just above the window. The prescription Kriesel ordered last week is stronger. Jeanne sleeps longer. She's more dopey. I look at my watch. Forty minutes, I think, which was how long ago she took her pill, just before we left the restaurant. She should be feeling better.

"Are you okay?" I ask.

She nods, and then says yes so I can hear.

I drive through the hot, crowded town. Women in shorts walk the streets with their blond-haired boys and girls. Businessmen in nice suits hurry in and out of buildings, across crosswalks. Old people shield themselves with purses or newspapers from the sun. At a stoplight I catch our reflection in a storefront window. An old Ford. A mother and daughter. Even a daughter slumped down, sick maybe or just sleeping. The light changes, and I continue home.

» » **Kathleen Smith**

Kathleen Rose Smith (Olemitcha Miwok/Mihilakawna Pomo) is a painter, traditional craftsperson, and writer. She grew up as a lively, creative youngster in the rural, agriculturally rich northern California town of Healdsburg. A graduate of the San Francisco Art Institute, she is presently represented by the Bear 'n Coyote Gallery in Jamestown, California.

» **Crab Louis and the Jitterbug**

Writing about my tribal foods brings back memories of thirty, forty, or fifty plus years ago. It gives me an added reason to spend more time with relatives, remembering together old times, hard times, great times, laying claim to our people's times, which include today.

In some ways the foods I grew up with reflect the times and the community I lived in, as well as my Indian heritage. My experience as a cultural demonstrator at Point Reyes National Seashore taught me that many people have little knowledge of California Indians and lots of mistaken ideas about California Indian foods. Sincere visitors would ask me about foods they heard were bitter, bland, or bizarre, foods that for them were only valid if stopped in time some two hundred years ago.

The foods of my ancestors that I know about are delicious, pungent, healthful, delicate, sweet, seasonal, fresh, preserved in salt, dried, jerked, and nutritious, and some, if not prepared properly, could be bitter, bland, or bizarre, and harmful. They have continuity with the past. Coastal foods belie my Bodega Miwok heritage, for instance, but they aren't stopped in time.

Which brings me back to childhood memories. My family loves seafood. So do I, except that when I was a child I was allergic to some kinds of seafood (a source of ridicule for a Bodega Miwok child) and could never remember which ones until it was too late.

I have outgrown my problem with seafood. Mamma always thought it was in my head anyway. Everyone else thought it was great; the more for them, they'd say. Even though I had problems with eating some seafood, I loved to go to the ocean and gather the foods the sea offers. Seaweed, shellfish, and other tidal inhabitants such as sea anemones and China shoes.

Crabmeat was one that I could eat. My sister June would make Crab Louis. As she would point out, she made it the best.

Geraldine Lucille, Gerri, Junie, June. The eldest in our family of four girls and four boys. She was sixteen years old when I was born in the winter of 1939. Junie was my hero, my role model, as we say these days. Like the zest of lemon in a glass of water, she brought refreshing elegance to the ordinary.

My bobby-soxed, beautiful sister seemed to fill the air with excitement and music and dancing. Her friends spilled through the house at 411 Foss Street. They were indulgent to me, the baby. I wanted to grow up to be just like Junie; to dance the jitter-bug, to have long, shiny, auburn-colored natural curls like her, and to put on lipstick like her, looking like Betty Grable. I couldn't see over the dining room table.

Junie had pride in who she was. At Geyserville School she played football, and she would beat up white boys who insulted Indian kids who lived with her on the Dry Creek Rancheria. She knew dad would defend her actions to the school administration.

When she was a littler girl at Geyserville, she won a footrace. The prize was a turkey. My mother was so happy.

Junie played the trumpet as good as Harry James. At Healdsburg

High School she played second trumpet, not because she was a girl, as I thought, but because Tom Ratchford was really better, June says. Her first horn was a cornet that cost $2.50. The second was a beautiful trumpet, a gift from her music teacher, Charles McCord. Mr. McCord got it from the San Francisco Symphony. It was such a fine instrument that Tommy Ratchford and Bill McCutchen, the other two trumpet players, would ask to borrow it.

When Junie graduated from high school, she was asked to play in a dance band. Mamma firmly said no. Instead, Junie went to work at Mare Island Naval Shipyard as a riveter. It was 1942. America had been at war for seven months. Junie played her trumpet occasionally at camp meetings, but when our brother Stanley wanted to learn a musical instrument a few years later, she gave him her beautiful trumpet.

The music that I love is the music introduced to me by Junie. The first song I learned to sing was "A Tisket, A Tasket" by teenager Ella Fitzgerald with Chick Webb's band. Junie's music was jazz, swing, blues, boogie-woogie, and jump tunes. The sounds of Duke, Count, Bix, Bunny, Benny, Billie, Coleman Hawkins, Johnny Hodges, Lester Young, the Teagardens, Valaida Snow, Jimmie Lunceford, Mildred Bailey. Well, you get the picture. Junie's music still swings. Floy doy. Floy doy.

During the 1940s, California Indians, Inc., was raising money to send delegates to Washington, D.C., to petition the federal government to act on California's unratified treaties. All eighteen treaties signed with California Indians in 1951 and 1952 were never ratified.

It wasn't until July 1963 when the case (or cases) was settled out of court during the Kennedy administration. Final payment was completed in 1972. Indians were paid a pittance for the land that had been taken from them. Many California Indians refused the money and sent it back.

Anyway, one of the ways the Indians in Sonoma County raised money for the delegate in their area, our uncle Manuel Cordova (Junie's Godfather, whom she called Nino), was to have dances where African American bands from the Bay Area would play. My folks bundled me up and took me along. I imagine it was here that I first learned to jitterbug like Junie.

Today, Junie works as an observer for archaeological projects, she is an area commissioner for Housing and Urban Development, and she still makes a mean Crab Louis.

June's Crab Louis

Serve with French bread.

Salad:

> Crabmeat from one precooked crab
> served over iceberg lettuce leaves
> One tomato, sliced
> One hard-boiled egg, sliced
> Marinated beets, to taste
> Asparagus spears, to taste
> Shrimp, optional

Dressing:

> 2 stalks fresh celery, grated
> 2 tablespoons dill pickle, grated
> About 1 cup cocktail sauce
> 2 cups mayonnaise
> Dash of Tabasco
> Dash of horseradish
> Juice from 1 lemon

» The Bitter and the Sweet

Prearranged marriage was common in the early days for my people, and so it was for my grandparents Steven Smith, Sr., of Bodega Bay and Mary (or Maria) Antone of Jenner. According to my Aunt Josie (Josephine Santos Wright, dad's half sister), the fathers of these two young people wished to form a "dynasty."

Before Steven and Mary were born, their fathers—William Smith, Sr., and James Antone, Sr.—were forced to participate in a terrible time in my people's history. Together with the rest of their people, as well as other tribes in Sonoma County, they were forced at gunpoint by American militia to walk to a relocation place in Lake County. Ever after, when recounting the old times, this was referred to as the Death March by my people.

Sadly, Bill Smith and Jim Antone were two of so few to return home several years later. When they and the others did return to their lands and homes, they found both were being occupied by Americans and the Asian nationals who were laborers. Both men, however, set out to rebuild their lives in the countries of their birth: the Bodega Bay coastal area south of Duncan's Point and the Jenner, Goat Rock, and Bridgehaven area near the mouth of the Russian River.

Picking up the pieces of shattered lives was both bitter and difficult. These two resilient men thought they could build an alliance from their own dwindled tribes, one Bodega Miwok, the other Jenner Pomo.

Great-grandfather Bill's first wife had died on the Death March. After he returned home, he met and married Rosalie Charles. Together they had ten children plus Rosalie's daughter from a previous marriage.

Bill Smith became a prosperous fisherman with his many sons. He was also a traditional clamshell disk bead maker, generous, loved, and respected by all who knew him.

Great-grandfather Jim Antone returned to his home to find Filipino nationals living there. Thereafter he had a hatred for all Asian people. Jim married Mary Pete. They had two sons and a daughter, my grandmother Mary. Before her marriage to Jim Antone, Great-grandmother Mary Pete was married to Tom Smith (Bill Smith's half brother). Mary and Tom had one son, John Smith.

Jim Antone was the traditional headman of his now-tiny band of survivors. He was also a celebrated grass game player whose songs would finally fail him as he lay dying in the shallow waters of Austin Creek, murdered after he returned from a successful game. When he didn't return home, his worried daughter Mary, whom he had disowned for marrying a Guamanian, went searching for him with her young son, my father, in a rowboat. They brought his body home, dragging it behind the boat. My father never forgot it.

An alliance would have helped to strengthen both tribes. A good idea, perhaps, but the fathers chose the wrong individuals. Steven and Mary did not like, let alone love, one another. The arranged marriage lasted four years, during which time my father, Steven, Jr., was born, as was a daughter named Dora who died in infancy. The death of the child was the end of the marriage.

Grandfather Steve never again married, but Grandmother Mary later married Joe Santos, a native of Guam, when my father was about six years old. Mary and Joe Santos had four daughters, Anne, Cecelia, Josephine, and Delores. Of all the children of my grandparents Steven and Mary, only Aunt Jo, now in her early eighties, survives.

This recounting of my people's history brings to mind festivals of other people who used to be tribes (ancient tribes, but not as old as California tribes) halfway around the world; of greens dipped in vinegar to remember the bitter tears shed by the ancestors for injustice suffered at the hands of the powerful; of apples dipped in honey and served at the beginning of the new year in order to have a sweet life.

I embrace both the bitter and the sweet, for both are a part of life; and I embrace life. No matter how much I would like to experience only the sweet times, a balance must come to pass.

Grandmother Mary knew much of the bitter and sweet in her life. She lived it all with grace and dignity. I, my siblings, all who came before me, are/were Bodega Miwok, Jenner Pomo, and Dry Creek Pomo, with just a dash of Yankee, a pinch of Russian, a liberal cupful of Portuguese, and even, it seems, a tad of the despised early-day Spanish through Great-grandmother Rosalie Charles.

The only exception to this in my lifetime, the only person who was all Indian, nothing else, was Grandma Santos, as we kids called her. I was about ten years old when she died. The thing I remember best about her was her quiet dignity, the big hats she wore to church every Sunday, her white hair rolled in a bun on top of her head, and her cooking.

She baked the best potato bread I ever tasted, baked in a cast-iron skillet in a woodburning oven. I wasn't the only one to love her potato bread. Aunt Josie told of the time she and Dad visited his uncle Angelo and was told by Angelo that they (the Smiths) learned to cook this wonderful bread from her mother, "Maria."

Rice pudding and bread pudding were also favorites. Blood sausage was a wonder. But the best, because of its visual impact, was stuffed chicken necks.

Start with a live chicken. A rooster is best, only because of the bigger comb and wattles, but a hen will do nicely, too.

Next, twist or wring the chicken's neck, then hang it by its legs, letting the blood drain into the neck. Pluck the feathers from the chicken. When blood is completely drained, chop off the neck with the head still attached, and remove the neck bone.

Clean the chicken by removing the intestines and gizzard. Take out the giblets, heart, and liver. Save these to grind in a meat grinder. Mix the ground-up giblets with spices, such as pickling spices. Add the mixture to the congealed blood. Stir to mix evenly. Put the giblet stuffing mixture into the neck and sew the skin at the bottom to keep the stuffing intact. Put the stuffed neck in a pot to boil. When the pot reaches a rolling boil, reduce the heat and cook in an uncovered pot until the chicken head and neck are done. It should take about 1 hour.

Serve as an hors d'oeuvre.

I rarely got to taste this delicacy because it ALWAYS was cooked for my dad at my house. Nevertheless, I was thrilled to see this wonderful dish served. Chicken and dumplings seemed so dull in comparison to a chicken neck, with its colorful wattles and comb.

» Abalone: A Precious Gift

On the first day of April the pilgrimage will continue. Once again dark figures will emerge out of the misty fog and move slowly to the sea. Men dressed head to toe in black will awkwardly descend, backward, into the icy surf, float a short distance on the ocean surface, then disappear. After what seems a long, long time, each will once more reappear, bringing with him, if blessed with good fortune, a precious treasure only the sea can give. Abalone.

Of course, the quest for abalone did not always begin on April Fool's day. This is a comparatively recent occurrence initiated by the fishing regulations of the State of California.

Abalone, arguably the most delectable of the foods of my people, has long been eaten by California's coastal and Channel Island Indians. When it was realized that restaurants would pay high prices for abalone, a new industry was created, as was the need to control the excesses of modern commerce. Unlike the days when abalone was gathered by small, hardy groups of individuals to feed their own families and friends, abalones, like so many of the seafood delicacies (such as turban snails and sea urchins), now need to be protected from becoming extinct because of the actions of people whose motivation for gathering them is dollars alone.

During my childhood, abalone could be picked off the rocks at low tide. Today, this is rarely so. Men and women, such as my Aunt Josie (Josephine Santos Wright) would search for abalone armed with a burlap sack and a handmade prying tool (a pointed stick, a tire iron, or anything else that would work), with which they could carefully remove the abalone without cutting its flesh. They would dress as warmly as they could, wearing woolen sweaters, long johns under loose-fitting cotton duck pants and rubber-soled canvas shoes. All this helped to shield them against the chilly waves, slippery rocks, and modern codes of propriety (their own ancestors had plied these same icy waters with no clothes whatsoever). Bemused white people thought they were fanatical or nuts.

Then the French ocean explorer Jacques Cousteau invented the wet suit, and this changed the method of abalone gathering. Because of the wet suit, the risk of drowning due to hypothermia was considerably reduced for those who did not grow up swimming in northern California's freezing ocean. True, one still has to be hardy and have strong lungs to dive into fifteen or so feet of buoyant seawater aided only by lead weights around the waist.

According to my nephew Steve Smith, removing abalone from the rocks on the ocean floor is actually easier than taking them from the tidal zone. They don't hold on so strongly to the rocks below the constant wave action.

Today the majority of abalone gatherers in California are non-Indians. However, Coast Miwok and other coastal Indians still head for the beach come April 1.

There are many ways to prepare abalone, truly one of the world's finest gourmet foods. The best I have tasted was prepared by Steve. He was kind enough to allow me to present it and other remembrances here. Now in his early forties, Steve, like all of his people, has spent a lifetime fishing and enjoying the ocean: "Just being at the ocean is so relaxing. Remembering the old times with Dad [Russell Smith] and Grandpa [Steven Smith, Jr.] makes it all worth it [the danger and cold]. It's renewing and makes the challenge of commuting and work less stressful just to remember those times."

They would make a fire on the beach to dry off. "Sometimes," he said, "Uncle Manuel and Grandpa would wait until there was only a bed of coals left, then place an 'ab' on the coals face down, still in its shell, and cover the abalone with coals and rocks." Later they would dig the cooked abalone out. The shell and guts would be burned off. Then they trimmed off all the charcoal and ate the chewy meat. "It was delicious." I, too, remember having abalone cooked this way on the beach when I was a youngster.

Steve also told me about someone he met who was a friend of my grandfather and great-uncles (the Smith brothers of Bodega Bay, who started the modern Sonoma County fishing industry). The friend said that the Smith brothers would make jerky out of abalone at Great-Grandfather Bill Smith's ranch at the Bay (Great-Grandmother Rosalie Charles Smith had already died by this time). Perhaps some of my cousins who lived at the Bay remember this, too.

Here's one of Steve Smith's several abalone recipes:

Remove the abalone from the shell and clean it. (If you are interested, carefully run the guts between your fingers, as sometimes there is a pearl inside. It is the same colors as the shell.)

Next, slice the cleaned abalone lengthwise ¼ to ⅜ inches thick. Steve also includes the "foot" (that part that attaches to the rock) in his slices. Have ready milk, two eggs, cracker crumbs, olive oil, dry white wine, and a wok.

Pound the abalone slices with a smooth, flat weight, such as a mallet or the iron used to pry the abalone from the rock. (Check the regulations of the California State Department of Fish and Game concerning a pry tool if you are unfamiliar with them. The measurements and other characteristics of the tool that may be used when removing abalone from the rocks are strictly regulated.) Pound the strips two or more times until the abalone is about to tear. Trim off and save the edges for chowder or fish bait. The edges are black, so they are easy to see and remove. If using them for chowder, scrape the black off. (I can share my mother's abalone chowder recipe another time.) All of this can be frozen to use later.

Soak the slices in a mixture of milk, eggs, and white wine. Use enough soaking mixture to cover all the slices. For two abalone, use 1½ cups of milk and two eggs, beaten together. Add ⅓ to ½ cup of dry white wine. Soak abalone in this.

Heat the wok to 375 to 400 degrees. Use enough olive oil to fry the abalone slices.

Grind up enough soda crackers in a blender to coat the abalone slices.

Remove the slices from the soaking mixture and roll them in the cracker crumbs, coating them completely. Then carefully place them in the hot oil. To test whether the oil is hot enough, put a small amount of cracker crumbs in the wok. When it's the right heat, the crumbs will bubble.

Turn the abalone slices once. Cook each side 35 to 40 seconds.

Season the abalone with fresh lemon juice, if desired. Serve with steamed rice and a fresh garden salad. If you are lucky enough to have some, decant and serve a bottle of my brother Bill's Pomo Ridge Dry Creek Valley Chardonnay for a meal you will remember for a long time.

Thank you, Steve, for generously sharing this delicious recipe and the memories. Thanks to the memory of Uncle Manuel and the other old ones who taught us the way by the example of their lives. Thanks to you mighty Pacific Ocean. May we, all of us who live on your shores and partake of your rich bounty, give you good gifts as you continue to give to us. Yah We.

» » Darryl Babe Wilson

Darryl Babe Wilson was born at the confluence of Fall River and Pit River at Fall River Mills, California, into two people: Atsuge-we on his father's side and A-juma-we on his mother's. He graduated from the University of California at Davis in 1992 with a major in English and is a student in the American Indian Graduate Division at the University of Arizona.

» Diamond Island: Alcatraz

November 21, 1989, 10:36 A.M.

There was a single letter in the mailbox. Somehow it seemed urgent. The address, although it was labored over, could hardly be deciphered— square, childlike print that did not complete the almost individual letters. Inside, five pages written on both sides. Blunt figures. Each word pressed heavily into the paper. I could not read it, but I could feel the message. "Al tr az" was in the first paragraph, broken and scattered, but there. At the very bottom of the final page, running out of space and evidently out of paper, he scrawled his name. It curved down just past the righthand corner. The last letter of his name, n, did not fit: *Craven Gibso*. It was winter 1971. I hurried to his home.

Grandfather Craven Gibson lived at Atwam, a hundred miles east of Redding, California, in a little shack out on the flat land. His house was very old and crooked, just like in a fairy tale. His belongings were few, and they, too, were old and worn. I always wanted to know his age and often asked some of the older of our people if they could recall when Grandfather was born. After silences that sometimes spanned more than a year, they always shook their silver-grey heads and answered: "I dunno. He was old and wrinkled with white hair for as long as I can remember. Since I was a child." He must have been born between 1850 and 1870.

Thanksgiving weekend, 1989. It is this time of year when I think about Grandfather and his ordeal. I keep promising myself that I will write his story down because it is time to give the island of Alcatraz a proper identity and a "real" history. It is easy for modern people to think that the history of Alcatraz began when a foreign ship sailed into the bay and a stranger named Don Juan Manuel de Ayala observed the "rock" and recorded it in a log book in 1775 (Ed Beyeler, *Alcatraz: The Rock* [1988], p. vii). That episode, that sailing and that recording, was only moments ago.

Grandfather said that long ago the Sacramento Valley was a huge freshwater lake, that it was "as long as the land" [from the northern part of California to the southern] and that a great shaking of an angry spirit within the earth caused part of the coastal range to crumble into the outer ocean. When the huge lake finally drained and the waves from the earthquake finally settled, there was San Francisco Bay, and there, in isolation and containing a "truth," was Diamond Island (Alcatraz).

We were in his little one-room house in Atwam. It is cold there in the winter, bitter cold. I arrived late in the evening, tires of the truck spinning up his driveway. The driveway was a series of frozen, broken mud holes across a field in the general direction of his home. The headlights bounced out of control. My old 1948 Chevy pickup was as cold inside as it was outside. The old truck kept going, but it was a fight to make it go in the winter. It was such a struggle that we called it Mr. Miserable. Mr. Miserable and I came to a jolting halt against a snowbank that was the result of someone shoveling a walk in the front yard. We expended our momentum. The engine died with a sputtering cough. The lights flopped out.

It was black outside, but the crusted snow lay like a ghost upon the earth and faded away in every direction. The night sky trembled with the fluttering of a million stars—all diamond blue. Wind whipped broken tumbleweeds across his neglected yard. The snow could not conceal the yard's chaos.

The light in the window promised warmth. With steam puffing from every breath, I hurried to his door. The snow crunched underfoot, sounding like a horse eating a crisp apple. The old door lurched open with a complaint. Grandfather's fatigued centenarian body was a black silhouette against the brightness—bright although he had but a single lamp without a shade to light the entire house. I saw a skinned bear once. It looked just like Grandfather. Short, stout arms and bowed legs. Compact physique. Muscular—not fat. Thick chest. Powerful. Natural.

Old powder-blue eyes strained to see who was out there in the dark. "Hallo, you're just the man I'm lookin' for." Coffee aroma exploded from the open door. Coffee. Warmth!

Grandfather stood back and I entered the comfort of his jumbled little bungalow. It was cozy in there. He was burning juniper wood. Juniper, cured for a summer, has a clean, delicate aroma—a perfume. After a healthy handshake, we huddled over steaming, thick, white cups made grey in the dim light. I think he was not totally convinced that I was there. The hot coffee was good. It was not a fancy aromatic Colombian blend, but it was so good!

We were surrounded by years of Grandfather's collections. It was like a museum. Everything was very old and very worn. It seemed that every part of the clutter had a history—sometimes a history that remembered the origin of the earth, like the dented pail of obsidian that he had collected from Glass Mountain many summers before, "just in case." He also had a radio that he was talked into purchasing when he was a young working man in the 1920s. The radio cost $124. I think he got conned by the merchant, and the episode magnified in mystery when he recalled that it was not until 1948 that he got the electric company to put in a line to his home. By that time he had forgotten about the radio, and he did not remember to turn it on until 1958. It worked. There was an odor of oldness—like a mouse that died, then dried to a stiffness through the years—a redolence of old, neglected newspapers.

The old person in the old house under the old moon began to tell the story of his escape from "the rock" long ago. He gathered himself together and reached back into a painful past. The silence was long, and I thought that he might be crying. Then, with a quiver in his voice, he started telling me the story that he wanted me to know.

"Alcatraz island, where the Pit River runs into the sea, is where I was born, long ago. Alcatraz, that's the white man's name for it. To our people, in our legends, we always knew it as Allisti Ti-tanin-miji [Rock Rainbow], Diamond Island. In our legends, that's where the Mouse Brothers, the twins, were told to go when they searched for a healing treasure for our troubled people long, long ago. They were to go search at the end of It A-juma [Pit River]. They found it. They brought it back. But it is lost now. It is said that the 'diamond' was to bring goodness to all our people everywhere.

"We always heard that there was a 'diamond' on an island near the great saltwater. We were always told that the 'diamond' was a thought or a truth, something worth very much. It was not a jewelry. It sparkled and it shined, but it was not a jewelry. It was more. Colored lights came from inside it with every movement. That is why we always called it Allisti Ti-tanin-miji."

With a wave of an ancient hand and words filled with enduring knowledge, Grandfather spoke of a time long past. In one of the many raids upon our people of the Pit River country, his pregnant mother was taken captive and forced, with other Indians, to make the long and painful march to Alcatraz in the winter. At that same time the military was "sweeping" California. Some of our people were "removed" to the Round Valley Reservation at Covelo, others were taken east by train in open cattle cars during the winter to Quapa, Oklahoma. Still others were taken out into the ocean at Eureka and thrown overboard into icy waters.

Descendants of those that were taken in chains to Quapa are still there. Some of those cast into the winter ocean at Eureka made it back to land and returned to the Pit River country. A few of those defying confinement, the threat of being shot by "thunder sticks," and dark winter nights of a cold Alcatraz made deadly by churning, freezing currents made it back to the Pit River country, too.

"I was very small, too small to remember, but my grandmother remembered it all. The guards allowed us to swim around the rock. Every day my mother swam. Every day the people swam. We were not just swimming. We were gaining strength. We were learning the currents. We had to get home.

"When it was time, we were ready. We left at darkness. Grandmother said that I was a baby and rode my mother's back, clinging as she swam from Alcatraz to solid ground in night. My grandmother remembered that I pulled so hard holding on that I broke my mother's necklace. It is still there in the water . . . somewhere." By pointing of a stout finger southward, Grandfather indicated where "there" was.

Quivering with emotion, he hesitated. He trembled. "I do not remember if I was scared," Grandfather said, thick, crooked fingers rubbing a creased and wrinkled chin covered with white stubble. "I must have been."

When those old, cloudy eyes dripped tears down a leathery, crevassed face, and there were long silences between his sentences, I often trembled too. He softly spoke of his memories.

Our cups were long empty, *maliss* (fire) needed attention. The moon was suspended in the frozen winter night—round, bright, scratched, and scarred—when Grandfather finally paused in his thinking. The old cast-iron heater grumbled and screamed when I slid open the top to drop in a fresh log. Sparks flew up into the darkness, then disappeared. I slammed the top closed. Silence again.

Grandfather continued, "There was not real diamonds on the island —at least, I don't think so. I always thought that the diamonds were not diamonds but some kind of understanding, some kind of good thought— or something." He shook a shaggy white head and looked off into the distance, into a time that was so long ago that the mountains barely remembered. For long moments he reflected, he gathered his thoughts. He knew that I "wrote things down on paper."

The night was thick. To the north a coyote howled. Far to the west an old coyote rasped a call to the black wilderness, a supreme presence beneath starry skies, with icy freedom all around.

"When I first heard about the 'diamond,' I thought it might be somehow a story of how we escaped. But after I heard that story so many times, I don't think so. I think there was a truth there that the Mouse Brothers were instructed to get and bring back long ago to help our people. I don't think that I know where that truth is now. Where can it be? It must be deep inside Ako-Yet [Mount Shasta] or Sa Titt [Glass Mountain]. It hides from our people. The truth hides from us. It must not like us. It denies us."

The one-as-old-as-the-mountains made me wonder about this story. It seems incredible that there was such an escape from Alcatraz. Through American propaganda I have been trained to believe that it is impossible to escape from this isolated rock because of the currents and because of the freezing temperature as the powerful ocean and the surging rivers merge in chaos. I was convinced—until I heard Grandfather's story and until I realized that he dwelled within a different "time," a different "element." He dwelled within a spirituality of a natural source. In his world I was only a foreign infant. It is true today that when I talk with the old people I feel like nilladu-wi (a white man). I feel like some domesticated creature addressing original royalty, knowing that the old ones were pure savage, born into the wild, free.

In his calm manner, Grandfather proceeded. "We wandered for many nights. We hid during the day. It is said that we had to go south for three nights before we could turn north. [They landed at San Francisco and had to sneak to what is now San Jose, traveling at night with no food until they could turn northward.] They were after us. They were after us all. We had to be careful. We had to be careful and not make mistakes. We headed north for two nights.

"We came to a huge river. We could not cross it. It was swift. My mother walked far upstream, then jumped in. Everybody followed. The river washed us to the other shore [possibly the Carquinez Straights]. We rested for two days, eating dead fish that we found along the river. We could not build a fire because they would see the smoke and catch us, so we must eat it [the fish] raw. At night we traveled again. Again we traveled, this time for two nights also.

"There is a small island of mountains in the great valley [Sutter Buttes]. When we reached that place, one of the young men climbed the highest peak. He was brave. We were all brave. It was during the sunlight. We waited for him to holler, as was the plan. We waited a long, long time. Then we heard: "Ako-Yet! Ako-Yet! To-ho-ja-toki! To-ho-ja-toki, Tanjan!

[Mt. Shasta! Mt. Shasta! North direction!]" Our hearts were happy. We were close to home. My mother squeezed me to her. We cried. I know we cried. I was there. So was my mother and grandmother."

Grandfather has been within the earth for many snows now. The volumes of knowledge that were buried with him are lost to my generation, a generation that needs original knowledge now more than ever if we are to survive as a distinct and autonomous people. Perhaps a generation approaching will be more aware, more excited with tradition and custom and less satisfied about being off-balance somewhere between the world of the "white man" and the world of the "Indian," and will seek this knowledge.

It is nearing the winter of 1989. Snows upon Ako-Yet are deep. The glaring white makes Grandfather's hair nearly yellow—now that I better recall the coarse strands that I often identified as silver. That beautiful mountain. The landmark that caused the hunted warrior 140 years ago to forget the tragic episode that could have been the termination of our nation, and, standing with the sun shining full upon him, hollered to a frightened people waiting below: "Ako-Yet! Ako-Yet! To-ho-jo Toki, Tanjan!"

Perhaps the approaching generation will seek and locate Allisti Titanin-miji within the mountains. Possibly that generation will reveal many truths to this world society that is immense and confused in its immensity. An old chief of the Pit River country, Charles Buckskin, said often: "Truth. It is truth that will set us free." Along with Grandfather, I think that it was a truth that the Mouse Brothers brought to our land from Diamond Island long ago, a truth that needs to be understood, appreciated and acknowledged.

Grandfather's letter is still in my files. I still can't read it, but if I could, I am sure that the message would be the same as this story that he gave to me as the moon listened and the winds whispered across a frozen Atwam during a sparkling winter night long ago.

» Gedin Ch-Lum-Nu / "Let It Be This Way"

In the teachings of my elders, such as Craven Gibson (he is from the Big Valley, which is in the heart of the Pit River country and claimed that he was born on Alcatraz Island in about 1855), there is the story of the time when the Hawaiian people were visiting the coast of California.

Their huge lumja-wi (canoe) broke apart on the rocks, and they struggled
to the shore. For many, many years they wandered the coast range and
the huge Sacramento—San Joaquin valley. Eventually their wandering
brought them inland, and they somehow found their way over the Sierra
Nevada range and into the land of my people, the A-juma-wi. The land of
my people lies in the northeastern corner of California. It is just south of
the Modoc. The Warner Range separates us from the Paiutes, Eagle Lake
and Mt. Lassen comprise the southern boundary, and Mt. Lassen and Mt.
Shasta are our western "cornerstones."

Upon viewing Bo-ma-rhee (the Fall River Valley), they immediately
fell in love with the earth and the people because both reminded them
so much of their homeland in Hawaii. They settled and mingled with
my people. Ako-Yet (Mt. Shasta) stood guard over them at night, A-juma
(the big river) sang to them as they dreamed and upon waking greeted
them with a fresh song. The winds moved softly through their spirits.
Fall brought many shades of rainbow colors to the earth. There was the
distinct call of the traveling goose, magic migrations of fleeting deer, and
splashing rivers of salmon.

Winter, something of a miracle to them, made the land clean and
cold, carpeted as if with powdered diamonds. Trees were fat and white
with heaps of snow that tumbled to earth in clouds of cold dust when
a branch was touched. Stars were frozen in the silent cold. Warm fire
was most welcome. Long nights were filled with songs and lessons and
legends and dreams.

Spring was a solid carpet of chartreuse, and the forest was an orches-
tra of blossom-flavored bird songs. The people prepared to live. They
readied to hunt *dok* (jackrabbits) and *do-se* (deer) and to work the big river
for *allis* (salmon) and *sal* (mussels). It was an exciting time of ceremonies
greeting another season and a preparation for the approaching phases of
all of the seasons of their lives. In this manner the people prepared to live
forever.

In summer they lounged in the dark shade of the tall forests or swam
in the churning, sometimes whispering river. They gathered *apas* (sweet
roots the size of your little finger growing just below the ground) in the
meadow and nuts from the pines. When they gathered *sal* and *ali wak-
qa* (freshwater clams), the Hawaiians remembered the shellfish of their
homeland. Often they sang their songs of the sea when pearls were beneath the ripples, rolling with the sands.

Happiness seemed to be everywhere.

Children laughed, dogs barked, elders dreamed, council gathered, lessons were remembered and taught by the fire. Life was good. But to the Hawaiians this was not home. It was very similar, except for the powdery winter snows. It was a good land. It was a good time of their life. They should have been happy.

But they were not dancing upon their own land. They were feasting, but not upon their own food. They were dreaming, but not dreaming the same dreams as they did in their homeland. Their children laughed and ran and played, but they were not doing all of these things upon their own earth.

There was something missing. They knew that they must return to their homeland or their songs and dances, their traditions and their customs, their language and their lessons would perish. Should these things disappear, they would have no purpose upon the earth—they would vanish, too!

This was a serious decision because some Hawaiians of A-juma-wi blood would have to go, and some A-juma-wis of Hawaiian blood would have to stay. Families were to be divided. Earth ceased breathing.

There was a thick quiet over the land. The smoke from the fire climbed into the sky, then spread across the blue, making a cloud canopy. Fire was worried. Ako-Yet leaned over the council and listened. The winds of the forest were silent, and the forest leaned and listened also. Birds and butterflies no longer fluttered in the brush but listened quietly. The hawk and the eagle hovered high over the council, suspended in time and space, and listened. The deer always listen, but on this day their listening was intense. You could touch their listening with the finger of your hand. Bear looked with small eyes upon the gathered people and Bear, too, listened. Earth was silent. Then, from the west, like a distant drum singing, a decision approached.

At the great council, as the A-juma-wi watched, the Hawaiians danced their dance of loneliness for their home. As they danced, they sang a song of the winds and of the pearls resting in the heart of the sea. They sang of swaying trees and of the bright and wholesome sun that bathed and warmed the earth. They sang of the moon rising over the vast ocean and of the silver trail that leads to the center of its heart. They sang of the vast panorama of stars that had no mountains to interfere with their vision. They sang of the earth, the people—and the children with flowers in their hair. They sang of the sterling laughter that can be heard from nations dwelling only upon their very precious land as children run with excited life beating in their hearts.

With one huge heart, the people of Hawaii and my people wept.

The decision was made. Gathered in council were the elders of the Hawaiians and the elders of the A-juma-wi. Their decision was painful but swift—like an arrow to the heart of your spirit.

In the silence, our silver-haired grandfather stood strong in the presence of all the world and in the face of the sun. His hair rippled in the soft winds, his cloudy eyes peered into an unknown time. With a trembling in his husky voice, he said loudly so everything could hear, "The Hawaiian people must return to their island home."

He hesitated for a moment. A tear came from his heart and watered the earth with a splash that the world still remembers. Softly he said, "Now is the proper time for the council to gather for the last time to make decisions."

It was decided that A-poni-ha (Cocoonman, one of the earth makers) would travel to the top of Ako-Yet and gather power so he could help the Hawaiians and those of mixed blood return to their warm islands of sand and sunshine. Cocoonman said, "Dupt-da!" which means, in our language, "We are going!"

He led the departing people to the land of the Kashaya Pomo. After explaining his purpose there and asking permission, he constructed a small fire. The Hawaiians, not knowing of the power within Cocoonman or the power within Ako-Yet, wondered how they were to return to their island, which was very far away. There was a vast ocean between them and their island. Their lumja-wi was smashed by the waves long ago, and it had washed away. They had no lumja-wi to replace it. Neither, it seemed, was Cocoonman concerned with a lumja-wi! How was a small fire and a song going to get them back to their homeland, as the council had instructed?

The A-juma-wi and some mixed-blood people stayed in our land with sad hearts. But animals and birds were permitted to follow the departing people as Cocoonman led them across the mountains, across the wide valley and over the ocean range to the land of the Kashaya Pomo. One animal and one bird, one of everything, was there to witness this event. They were the messengers back to their own "people" so that all of life would know this story.

Cocoonman sang a little song to the spirits of the universe and to the spirits that dwell far, far beyond the farthest stars. He sprinkled into the fire the blossoms of the sage and the pollen of the pine, the flowers of the valley and the perfume of the plum, the dust of the grasses and the lichen from the highest rock of the great mountain Ako-Yet.

From that little fire there arched a beautiful, intense rainbow. It reached from the land of the Kashaya Pomo to the heart of the islands known as Hawaii. It was powerful. It was beautiful. The Hawaiians were frightened, as they had not yet fully understood the power of the song, the power of the mountain and the land, the power of Cocoonman, or the power of the final decision of the council.

Cocoonman invited the Hawaiians to walk across the rainbow and return to their homeland. They dared not! Cocoonman then walked upon the rainbow to show them it was solid and firm. They refused!

His duty, decided by the council, was to assist the Hawaiian people back to their homeland—safely, not full of fright. He sang a song and dreamed a dream, and in a brilliant flash his dream gave him instructions.

Cocoonman positioned himself and extended his left hand toward Hawaii—to where the end of the rainbow touched the earth. Then he extended his right hand back across the land of the Kashaya Pomo and said, "Gedin ch-lum-nu." In the language of my precious people this means, "Let it be this way."

Instantly a land the width of two grown men removed itself from the earth and lay across the waters, a bridge breathing upon the ocean to the end of the rainbow. Cocoonman then walked upon this bridge to show the gathered people that it was sturdy. They could walk upon earth, but they dared not walk upon the rainbow for the fear of falling through. Still, they were not certain about the end of the bridge, whether it reached their islands.

Cocoonman then instructed Yas (Weasel) to walk with them to their home. Yas fashioned a flute from a reed that he found in the nearby stream, tuned it to his satisfaction, and began playing soft music. Cocoonman tended the fire and continued singing the song to all of the powers of all of the universe.

As Yas played, he danced, and his dance led him to the rainbow bridge, and he floated upon it like a hawk landing upon a pine limb. He then walked across that beautiful bridge high in the sky. As he walked the rainbow path, he played the flute. As he walked the rainbow path, the

Hawaiians walked the land bridge far below, without fear. And the music that came from the flute was so beautiful that it was heard all around the world.

As Yas moved into the distance, the music dimmed. Soon the music could be heard growing louder. Yas returned. He stepped off the rainbow and placed the reed back in the stream so it would continue to grow beautiful music forever.

The Hawaiians were safely home. The land bridge returned to the mainland. The rainbow returned to the fire. The Kashaya Pomo returned to their homes. The birds and animals returned to their domains, and the songs and the music returned to silence and peace.

Alone, Cocoonman glided like the thick shadow of a great eagle. He floated across the snow-capped mountains and over the valleys, observing everything. He remembered again and again the departure of the people. Something soft caught in his throat.

He settled at the base of Ako-Yet, folded up there, knelt before Mis Misa[1] and, because he had, for the second time in his existence, accomplished the impossible, trembled.[2]

A very old Grandfather of the Pit River Nation, Craven Gibson, told me this story in 1971 under an immeasurable vastness of frozen stars in the heart of winter (this has also been told by Ramsey Bone Blake and Wes Cline). He had always wanted to go to wade in the warm waters of Hawaii and look for pearls, especially when the winter winds whipped through the cracks of his little home and howled during the winter night like a pack of desperate wolves. He said that we are all related, the Hawaiians and the A-juma-wi, and to prove it there is a way:

> Take a handful of earth from Hawaii
> and rub it on the A-juma-wi
> and the dirt and the skin will remain the same hue.

1. Mis Misa is the small power that dwells deep within Ako-Yet. It balances the earth with the universe and the universe with the earth. Like a pendulum, it shifts each time Great Wonder stirs the vastness with that immense yet invisible ja-pilo-o (canoe paddle). As is its assigned purpose, Mis Misa keeps us in balance with all that there is.

2. The first time Cocoonman "accomplished the impossible" was when he helped make the world. At this point he realized that he had received, as a gift upon his birth, an amazing power to create.

Take a handful of earth from A-juma-wi
and rub it on the Hawaiian
and the dirt and the skin will remain the same hue.

» Et-Wi

With the words of an old grandmother, "A-poni-ha, me-moo-isch-e
(Great Spirit, we are your little children)," swimming within my spirit,
my twin boys, Hoss and Boss, who were three years old, went with me
to the home of "Grampa" Ramsey Bone Blake. Jo-ji (Bone) is one of his
real names, but his father worked for a man named Blake. That is how
his father acquired that name. Grampa lived in a little apartment between
Fall River Mills and McArthur overlooking the Pit River. To the north,
across the flat valley and above the mountains, Ako-Yet (Mt. Shasta) stood
strong, heavy, and silently frozen.

Sun was white gold and frigid. Wind moved. Leaves scurried in a
swirl stirred by an invisible finger in the driveway. The engine of our old
truck growled. It did not want to labor today. We did not want to labor
either, so we went to Grampa's for a talk—and cookies.

We had just killed a buck and took some back-strap to Grampa. The
old ones of our lives appreciate good meat, and they prefer the heart,
liver, and back-strap of the deer. With fried potatoes, greasy gravy, and
biscuits, back-strap is so delicious.

He was at his plain little table in his worn apartment. Instant coffee
and a spoon were on the table, and steaming water was on the stove. He
had just had breakfast and was reading from his bible. His countenance
was one of surprise and happiness to see us, but there was a thickness to
his manner. Somehow I knew that he wanted to talk. He always called it
"Talk that doesn't mean anything anyhow." But I always delighted in listening to him because he had so much to say. It was not gossip or news, it
was a lesson.

After shaking his hand (which was like shaking the hand of a stout
thirty-year-old weight lifter), I accepted a cup of instant coffee, and while
the twins rolled around on the carpet and bounced off of his bed like two
little cubs, we talked.

He put both hands on the table and opened them as one would open a book, softly but deliberately, expecting the book to fall open at just the page that one searched for. With almost sad gray eyes he looked out his window into a past that had no limit of time and into a future that had no boundary. His old eyes did not focus on anything in particular but saw life in its totality. He was solemn. His bottom lip trembled slightly and his hands vibrated just a little. Silence was thick all around us.

Then he smiled, and his countenance, which often reminded me of a balding and white-headed Elmer Fudd, softened. Making an excuse for me not to fully understand what he was about to deliver, his eyes twinkled and he said, "Many people don't believe what I'm telling. It's true. When I was young and years before I was a buckaroo, I dreamed of being medicine man, powerful doctor. I wanted *elam-ji* (the spirit power) so I could tame many *damaa-gomis* and have my damaa-gomis capture and tame *dini-how-wis*.[1] In this way I would be strong medicine doctor. I would have power. I wanted powerfulness. White Horse Bob taught me one song. The one Quon [Silver Fox] sang when he made world. That's White Horse Bob's power, his dini-how-wi, that song.

"I tried. I got cleansing and went to Rainbow Falls. Ran there early in morning. I talked, but spirit did not answer me. I got 'nother cleansing and traveled to *ene-hal-ewi* [the falls in the deep canyon near Fall River Mills]. I got cleansing again and ran to *ipaa-ka-ma* [Bald Mountain], to the top. I talked, I hollered, but again spirit did not answer. Grandmother told me to get ceremony, then go to Sa-tit [Medicine Lake] to stay until power claim me. Maybe I returned too soon. Maybe I was not strong enough. Maybe I was shy.

"White Horse Bob said get purification and go into Pit River Canyon [between Little Valley and Big Valley]. There I would find cave. It would not be big cave. It would be small one. That place would not look like place where power lives, but it is. It will fool you.

"He said I would find log hanging across but high above river. It would not reach the other side, so I had to run length of the tree and jump as far as I could to reach the other side. I needed to reach cave. I needed dini-how-wi.

"White Horse Bob said there would be big spider living in there. It

1. *Damaa-gomis* and *dini-how-wis* are spirit helpers of my people of the extreme northeastern corner of California. They bring both luck and power. It is said that the life force is not strong if it does not have this power.

would be curl up in corner near the roof. It would have red mark on its belly. That is how I would know this was proper place.

"After my old people cleansed me, I found the cave and crossed over on the dangerous tree, like White Horse Bob said to do. I was brave. Something pulled me into the canyon, into the cave. Spider was there. When first I entered, it was dark, but there was enough light to see after a little while. Spider was there. It was not curl up but was hanging in the net. There was a red mark on its belly, just like White Horse Bob said it was to be.

"The spider did not like me in the cave, and cave did not want me, so I went to Big Valley for few days 'wandering' before I went home. For my dini-how-wis I chose ro-nee-wee (thunder), ch-ar-te-see (power), and et-wi (eagle). I wanted a white eagle. Just somehow white eagle seemed power.

"I prayed, Babe. I prayed. I prayed. I did everything like I was told, but I didn't have the strength to have power. They told me to dive in Jema-halo-tiwiji [Great White Owl, or Burney Falls]. And I did. They told me to fast. And I did. They told me to be a dreamer. And I dreamed dreams. But still I was not medicine man. I did not have the power to tame dini-how-wi or damaa-gomi.

"It seemed like I was sick or something—dizzy. There was something that wasn't right. There was something wrong, and I did not know what it was. I didn't think about womans. I didn't think about drinks. I didn't think about bad things but about good things. Still . . .

"The day I knew I would not have power came. I was home and the door open. Sky was clear. It was just clear. There was no clouds everywhere.

"Lightning flashed. Scared me. Then thunder pounded the sky—I tried to break it! Through the door I could see lightning flash far past the valley. Then it flashed far past the mountains. Goin' away. It was fading. Thunder beat sky, but it moved away. It went across valley like lightning, and it rolled, heavy, down the canyon. It faded to quietness.

"Like a spirit, a clear shadow—kind of like the clean window—white eagle landed in the door. It folded wings and looked from side to side. It looked all around but did not look at me. Et-wi had yellow eyes with black in the middle and yellow feet. The rest of it looked like white eagle, but it had small black feathers above each eye—like eyelash. Claws made a scrape and thud as they grabbed the boards on the porch.

"It said nothing. It just looked, but not at me. Then it turned and slowly looked over its left shoulder. With a movement it was in the air, gliding across the valley. Like the thunder and lightning, it faded. It made it across the valley. I was still looking through door. It glided up to go over mountains over in the west—and disappeared . . . just like thunder and the lightning.

"It was then I knew that I would never be medicine man. I could not have power. I was rejected. Power did not want me. I did not have strength overcome it."

It seemed I held my breath as he spoke. After a long silence, we got a fresh cup of coffee and small-talked. He got the twins two more cookies each and a small glass of milk. When we were finished with our refreshments, we left Grampa for our home in the solitude of the Pit River Canyon—there on the western end under the Hat Creek rim.

He left some stories with me that I am recording for my children, so they will somehow know the strength and conviction that it takes to become a person of power—a medicine person. And perhaps they will not skim across the earth, taking titles like "pipe carrier" or "medicine man" or "power person" from people who have no authority to issue them. Power and medicine are not elements of life that are issued by people, they are pure and precious pieces of a great mystery that must be earned, deserved, and maintained—and something one is born to receive.

During the full moon of October 1984, Grampa left us. Like the white eagle, his spirit floated over the valley, casting no shadow.

Before There Was Something, There Was Nothing: The Creation
(As told and retold by many elders of our nation)

One way of saying *Coyote* in my language is *Jamol*. In this story, Quon calls Coyote Jamol. But outside of the direct quotations from Quon, I use *Coyote* because it is a universal known to everybody.

In the lessons and legends of my people dwelling beside the whispering waters of It A-juma (the Pit River, in northeastern California), there is a telling of how the universe and all that we know of and all that we cannot possibly know was created by a song of Quon (Silver Fox) and made manifest by the dance of both Quon and Jamol.

This lesson is also one of how jealousy and vanity entered the universe and how those two elements are the most damaging to the earth and to the people today.

There are many renditions of this lesson. Often a lesson can be tailored to fit a specific event or a series of events that unfolds before us. Sometimes the telling relates to an incident in a far distant past that may relate to something in a far distant future. Being "complete," the lessons are eternally fresh and continually useful. This lesson begins with simple beauty:

Before there was something, there was nothing.

There was a vastness, a void. It was not a darkness void. It was a vastness that was silent. It was extremely quiet. Nothing.

A thought made itself present in the vastness.

The thought created itself into a voice. It was but a single voice in all of the vastness of everything that we know and everything that we cannot know.

The thought thought and thought. Finally it spoke, saying, "I will be somebody or something. I will be happier *being*."

The thought decided to become a form and to make itself into the form of Quon. Like the stars that seem to pop out just as the sun is setting, creating a pattern here and a string of broken and scattered diamonds over there, Quon began to take shape. The thought began to have a being.

Over a period of ten million years, the thought had manifested itself into a form. It was Quon, the Silver Fox. Silver Fox is the power that is responsible for all that is good within the universe today.

Dwelling within the vastness of all that there is, and being all alone, Quon grew lonely. So, one day, he thinks, "I thought myself into being, maybe I can think up somebody else, someone that I can talk to. I am tired of being lonely. It would be good to talk to somebody and to maybe sing a song. Yes, I will think up somebody. I won't be lonely anymore."

Quon thought and thought. Unknown to him, he had created another being with his thought, and that being was traveling through time and space, going no particular place and with no particular destination, just wandering. Quon and the other being wandered the vastness for ten million years. Then one day, as they are not expecting it and they are each walking backward looking over the path that they had traveled, they bump into each other!

They spin around, frightened and scared and scared and frightened, and look each other in the eye. Quon said, "Who are you? You look almost like me, but who are you? And where are you going?"

Old Coyote said, "I am Jamol. Long ago I was nothing. Then I materialized into something. For a long time there was only silence. I did not know I could talk until I bumped into you just now. Where did my voice come from? I am Jamol and I am just traveling—no particular place to go, so I'll just go everywhere at any time. Who are you, and where did you come from? And . . . where are you going?

"I am Quon. I have been thinking. I can create things from my thinking. I thought about creating somebody so I could talk with them and there would not be just silence in this vastness. I travel around and think. Since you look kind of like me, you must be the person I thought up so we could talk. Let's travel and talk."

Jamol said, "Okay, but where will we travel to? Do you know a place where we can go?"

"Yes," said Quon. "I know all of the places of all that there is. I have dwelled here for ten million years, and I have traveled everywhere."

Old Coyote looks long at Quon out of the side of his eye. He is not sure about Quon being ten million years old, since Coyote was only five million years old. If all of this is true, thought Coyote, then Quon may have created me with his thought power. But that cannot be, since I have a stronger thought than Quon. Just maybe I created Quon with my thought and he is trying to steal the power to create from me. But Old Coyote knew all along that he did not acquire the power to create.

At this precise point in history, jealousy and vanity entered the picture. They hosted doubt, resentment, pain, and confusion. Coyote saw these things and wrapped them in a blanket so Quon could not see them and tucked them in the little "cut" in his ear.

These beings wandered across eternity. They went here and there, looking over all that there was not. They talked, and Coyote always tried to figure out how Quon created things with his thought power. Old Coyote knew that he did not have that special creative power, so he wanted to steal it from Quon.

They stopped and sat down to rest, looking over all that there was not for a million years. Then Quon said, "Let's make something!" Old Coyote gives a big yawn, looks at Quon out of the corner of his eye, and grumbles, "We can't make something outta nothin'." Doubt made itself present.

"But I thought myself into being, and I thought you into being. Here I am, and there you are. We are something. We will create something by thinking. Let's make something shiny. Let's think!" Quon set himself to thinking. Coyote went to sleep, snoring very loudly. Quon took Coyote's tail and stuffed it in Coyote's mouth to muffle the sound since it interfered with his thought.

Coyote slept for a million years as Quon thought for a million years. Then, far off in the distance there was something, and it shined in the vastness! The vastness was almost like a summer evening when the sun has dropped below the horizon of the western mountains and there is a silver darkness everywhere.

Quon kicked Coyote awake. "Don't look, but far over there is something, and it is shiny. Don't look or it might disappear."

Old Coyote yawns. Then he wakes up with a snap. "*Something!* Where?"

"Far over there to the left, but don't look," Quon cautioned. "It might get scared and leave."

Quon, sitting between Coyote and Something was busy thinking and could not watch Coyote. Coyote looked far around Quon and looked far into the distance. Yes! There it is. Something!

Coyote blinked so he could get a better look. Bing! Something was gone. Coyote saw it vanish. Quon could feel it leave his thought. Quon looked at Coyote. Coyote was lying on his belly with his arms crossed in front of him, relaxed and looking straight ahead, ears up, as if he were looking for a squirrel or a rabbit. Quon knew what had happened.

At this moment in history, disobedience and deception were born.

Quon was upset, but he said, "Let's try it again. This time, Jamol, don't look!"

Old Coyote promised not to look. Quon began thinking again. Coyote did not go to sleep this time. It took another million years of thinking before Something appeared far to the left. There it was! "Don't look, Jamol, but Something is back, Quon whispered. Don't look."

Coyote squeezed his eyes shut as hard as he could. Quon continued to think. "It is moving closer, and it is growing larger—but don't look, Jamol," Quon cautioned. Coyote did not look but squeezed his eyes even tighter because he wanted to see what Something looked like, and he knew that if he looked Something might disappear again. He did not look. "It is almost here. Here it comes. I got it! Now, Jamol, you can look. I have it. I think it is a mist."

While Coyote has his eyes closed tightly, the doubt that he wrapped in the blanket and hid in his ear was buzzing around in his brain like an annoying housefly, buzzing here and there, landing on anything, having no direction, just going.

When Coyote opened his eyes, doubt had caused him to think that Quon did not know how to handle Mist, so he grabbed for it.

"Lemme havit!" demanded Coyote.

"No!" hollered Quon. "You don't know how to care for it."

"Yourgonna dropit and it'llbreak!" said Coyote in a mean voice.

They began wrestling and shoving. Pretty soon Mist floated out of the hands of Quon. Coyote had Quon's arms pinned against his sides in a bear hug. Mist was floating down . . . and down . . . dangerously down!

When Coyote tried to get a better grip on Quon, Quon wiggled free and just as Mist was about to strike nothingness and break, Quon reached far down under Mist and caught it softly. Mist was safe.

"What will we do now?" asked Coyote.

"Let's make it grow."

"Howwegonnado that?" demanded Coyote.

"Let's sing. Let's sing and dance," said Quon, still holding Mist softly. So they sang and they danced, and they danced and they sang. Their heartbeat was the drum and their music was the silence. They danced and they danced and they danced. They sang and they sang and they sang.

Pretty soon, as Quon was holding Mist in his hands and they were dancing in a vast circle, Mist began to have substance. It took on a more physical form. It turned almost into a jelly. It took a shape. It was round. It was clear, and it was round, and it began to have texture. They sang and they danced. Pretty soon they stopped.

"Whattlewedonow?" demanded Coyote.

By now Mist had taken on the form of soft dough that only requires kneading and then baking before it feeds the spirit of the heart. It was pliable. It could be formed.

"Let's put it right down here," said Quon as he carefully placed it in front of but below them. It stayed there. "Now let's sing and dance some more."

Coyote couldn't see the point of it, but he sang and danced some more. "Don't look down, Jamol. Don't look until I tell you to look."

They sang and danced in a circle around Something. For a million years they sang and danced. Something began to grow and grow. "Look now, Jamol. Look. We have made it grow. It is big now."

Old Coyote looked. He saw that it grew very large. "Whattlewedonow?" wondered Coyote—mostly to himself.

"Let's jump on it and see if it will hold us," said Quon. So they jumped down on it. "Dance! Sing!" said Quon. They danced and sang. They sang and danced, and the dust began to fly. Where there were pieces of flint, they made sparks as they danced. Some of the dust was white, and some of the dust was all the colors of the rainbow. They danced and they sang. The dust flew and there were sparks.

Pretty soon they both grew weary. They stopped. "I needadrink" demanded Coyote. So near where they were standing Quon made a lake, and between two mountains he made a river. Coyote looked in the lake, which was like a mirror, saw himself, and immediately fell in love.

While Coyote was drinking and falling in love with himself, the sparks moved farther and farther away, the dust-of-many-colors moved farther and farther away.

"Whattlewecall this place?" asked Coyote.

"We'll call it earth," answered Quon. "And all of the sparks and the dust will be the stars." And so it was.

"Whattlewedonow?" asked Coyote.

"Let's make a lot of things," answered Quon. "You think up things and I will think up things. We can make a lot of things."

Old Coyote looked at Quon out of the corner of his eye, knowing all along that he could not "create" with thought but wishing that he could. So Coyote said, "You go ahead and make things for a while. I'll catch up." Coyote knew he had the power to change things, but he knew also that he did not have the power to create.

Coyote hoped that he was better-looking than Quon, but the reflection from the placid lake did not support his hope. He dismissed that with a self-explanation that the fish in the water must be distorting his image, so he followed behind Quon. Every time Quon made something, Coyote changed it because he thought Quon had made it defective in the first place. And Old Coyote knew that if he made something, he would make it perfect. Old Coyote was convinced that every time he changed a creation of Quon it was for the better.

Thus the universe and all that we know and all that we cannot possibly know was created by a song and a dance. It is said that Coyote made some of the people of our nation, but only a few claim his spirit as their own.

Still, today we see the Coyote-spirit that was made devoid of creativity but with the power to change—the power to change everything. Some things Coyote-spirit changes many times. Every time Coyote-spirit changes something, he is not satisfied with it, so he has to change it again. But, far back in his thinking, Coyote-spirit is very happy that Quon has somebody to follow after him, changing everything for the better.

Today, when my people see the corporation-spirit changing the rivers, changing the mountains, changing the animal and people populations and destroying the forests, we ask them what they are doing. They always say that they are changing it to make it better. They must change the river because it is for the best. It was wrong in the first place. They must cut down the forests because too many trees are not good for each other or for the animal life dwelling there. They must change the animal and people populations because they know best how to do these things and they have every reason to believe that they know best how to make the world better. They must move and remove mountains because they are all in the wrong place. Thus it goes. Jealousy and Vanity changing everything—for the best . . . devoid of the power to create, overflowing with the power to destroy, empty of the emotion of remorse.

» **Splashes of Red**
Autumn 1867, Tuwutlamit Wusci[1]

The odor of scorched gunpowder
    filled the air
In the morning
    it lay in soft, blue clouds
        over the earth of my people
    in the high desert
South of Modoc, west of Paiute

As the Great Powers of the seasons of our world
    move the goose and the salmon and the deer to migrate
So, too, that awesome power moves
    my people to gather
        for the last time before the long winter
To talk and to plan
    for the future and for the future of the children
And so it is

They gathered there in fear
    knowing the soldiers were tracking them
Yet they obeyed that great power
    and gathered as is the custom of the ages

They smelled the sweat of the horses
    and of *weet-la* (devils)
They heard the distant report
    of the rifle

Yet they listened to the life of nature
    moving all around them
And they gathered
    at tuwutlamit wusci they gathered
    . . . for the last time before the long winter

1. The Infernal Caverns near Likely, California, where my grandmother was born. At Infernal Caverns, September 1867, the military of the United States fell upon a gathering of my people and committed unpardonable crimes.

They did not think
>   about the Paiute woman
>   who slept with the soldiers
>   . . . And they told her of the gathering at tuwutlamit wusci

>   . . . And they came on sweating horses
>   with their rifles in their hands

Frightened
>   young mother ran towards the safety of tuwutlamit wusci
>   . . . Too late

When she looked back
>   there was blood in her tracks
But she felt no pain
>   for the pain was not hers to bear
Quickly she took the cradleboard from off of her back
>   and lay it in the sunshine of autumn

The blood in her tracks—
>   the infant on her back
>   . . . shot once through the neck
>   once, but forever

With her hands she dug a little grave
>   in a frightened crevasse of the trembling mountain
>   . . . And dried her tears with the dust of the sweet earth

She placed the eternal bundle
>   In that shallow effort
>   covered it with stones and a little flower growing nearby
>   . . . And she, in fear—and a broken heart
>   cried, among the splashes of red, Autumn, 1867 . . .

» Dancing

Floyd Buckskin, Jr., was dancing in the Dana Forest in his eagle cloak
during the summer. I heard the comments mentioned in the text and
wrote this note down so that the thought would not be lost.

On a summer day he was in the dreaming forest, et-wi (eagle)
Elam-ji (his spirit) moved him to dance with the music in nature

Neh-llah-deh-wi (white man) saw him

Soon we learned that white man said
      to his friends and those he could gather across the earth
          as they laughed
      he saw an "Indian" dancing alone—maybe possessed by a demon

In our lessons we learn
      it is the custom of nature to dance with the music of the universe

On a summer day he was dancing in the forest, et-wi
His spirit caused him to move with the music of the universe

As his spirit continued to flow with the power that balances *all*,
      he wondered:

              "How is it that I could dance alone?

              "How, alone, when all of the universe is wrapped
                  so delicately around us each
                  so full of purpose?"

Acknowledgments

The editor gratefully acknowledges permission to reprint the following previously published material:

Janice Gould, "Coyotismo," "Children Who Never Departed," "Doves," "History Lesson," "We Exist," "When Winter Hits Lake Erie," "To Speak Your Name," "Blackbirds," "Three Stories from My Mother," "Questions of Healing," "Last Journey," and "Beneath My Heart" from *Beneath My Heart*, by Janice Gould, published by Firebrand Books, Ithaca, N.Y. Copyright © 1990 by Janice Gould. By permission of the poet and the publisher.

Wendy Rose, "If I Am Too Brown or Too White for You" from *The Half-Breed Chronicles and Other Poems*, published by West End Press, 1985, reprinted 1992. By permission of the poet and the publisher. "For the Angry White Student Who Wanted to Know if I Thought White People Ever Did Anything Good for 'the Indians'" from *Going to War with All My Relations: New and Selected Poems*, by Wendy Rose, published by Northland Publishing. Copyright © 1993. All rights reserved. Used with permission.